Justice and Human Rights
in Islamic Law

Justice and Human Rights
in Islamic Law

Gerald E. Lampe
Editor

Published in Celebration of the Silver Anniversary of the
Shaybani Society of International Law

INTERNATIONAL LAW INSTITUTE

This book is published and distributed by the International Law Institute. For further information or to place an order:

> Publishing Office
> International Law Institute
> 1615 New Hampshire Avenue, NW
> Washington, D.C. 20009
> 202-483-3036
> 202-483-3029 (fax)
> E-mail: pub@ili

INTERNATIONAL LAW INSTITUTE®

The International Law Institute is a private, not-for-profit organization, established in 1955 at Georgetown University. Independent since 1983, the ILI's activities have expanded to encompass scholarly research, publishing, and practical legal training and technical assistance on many aspects of international legal and economic policy and practice. Over 6,000 lawyers and other officials from 155 countries have participated in ILI courses.

THE SHAYBANI SOCIETY OF INTERNATIONAL LAW

The Shaybani Society is dedicated to expanding the understanding of Islamic law and to providing a forum for discussion of current legal issues in the Middle East. The Society resides at the International Law Institute as an affiliated organization. To correspond with the Society, contact the Institute at the address above.

The Executive Committee of the Shaybani Society

President: Majid Khadduri	George Naifeh
Vice-President: Don Wallace, Jr.	Edmund Ghareeb
Secretary: Gerald Lampe	Don Perez
Treasurer: James Knight	Stuart Kerr
Thomas Mallison	

ISBN: 0-035329-84-X

Copyright ©1997 by the International Law Institute. All rights reserved. No part of the book may be reproduced in any form \or by electronic or mechanical means including electronic storage and retrieval systems without written permission of the author, except by a reviewer, who may quote brief passages in a review.

Table of Contents

Preface vii
Gerald Lampe

History of The Shaybani Society of International Law ix
Majid Khadduri

Justice and Human Rights in Islam 1
Muhammad Tal'at Al-Ghunaimi

The Conception of Justice: Western and Islamic 23
Liaquat Ali Siddiqui

Justice in the Islamic Shari'a 43
Muhammad Fathi Al-Dirini

The Concept of Justice and Human Rights in Islam 51
Noor ul-Amin Leghari

The Concept of Justice in Islamic Jurisprudence 65
Ali Bardakoglu

Islamic Criminal Law 79
Muhammad Abu-Hassan

Jihad as a Concept of Just War 91
Majid Khadduri

Appendix: Constitution of the Shaybani Society
    of International Law 96

Preface

The papers which follow are the result of a series of seminars and discussions held at the International Law Institute in Washington, D.C. and elsewhere in the U.S. in celebration of the Twenty-Fifth Anniversary of the establishment of the Shaybani Society of International Law in the United States. The objective in holding the seminars and discussions, entitled "Conceptions of Justice: Western and Islamic" and featuring prominent thinkers, jurists, and legal practitioners from nine Islamic countries, was not solely to highlight the accomplishments of the Shaybani Society over the past quarter of a century, but primarily to promote mutual respect and understanding between the two distinct legal traditions. This is very much in keeping with the objectives of the Shaybani Society itself "to promote the study of Islamic law, especially the law relating to the international field" and "to foster, in particular, the study of international law relating to the Islamic world," and these were stated in the Society's Constitution in recognition of the fact that mutual respect and understanding can only be achieved when the people of the West and those of the Islamic world are adequately informed about one another. As far as we have been able to ascertain, the Shaybani Society remains the only organization in the United States which devotes itself to promoting the study of international law as it relates to the Islamic world.

The subject of justice was selected because it is of central importance in both areas of the world and because it is a broad subject which encompasses, among other things, the concepts of democracy, human rights, the rule of law, and criminal law. These topics were the principal themes of the discussions and of the papers contained in this book, and they led to meaningful dialogue between the American and Muslim participants and helped them find common ground between the two value systems.

Professor Majid Khadduri presents in the first paper a history of the Society. This is followed by papers which focus on the topics of justice and human rights in Islamic law by Professors Tal'at Al-Ghunaimi, Liaquat 'Ali Siddiqui, Muhammad Fathi Al-Dirini, Noor ul-Amin Leghari, and Ali Bardakoglu, then by a paper by Judge Muhammad Abu-Hassan on Islamic criminal law, and finally by a paper by Professor Khadduri on *jihad* as a concept of just war. It is important to note that Professors Muhammad Ben Maazouz, Abu-Bakr Mustapha, and Muhammad Bin Sa'd al-Rashid presented papers at the seminars and made valuable comments, but these were not submitted for inclusion in this volume.

The Silver Anniversary celebrations and this book are as much a tribute to Professor Khadduri as to the Society itself. It was he who took the initiative to establish the Shaybani Society in the United States, and it was he who undertook to translate Shaybani's *Siyar* into English and to inform the American public about Shaybani's contributions to International Law. Furthermore, Professor Khadduri has served as President of the Society since its establishment in this country and has been the leading force behind its activities, working in close cooperation with the members of the Executive Committee of the Shaybani Society.

This book and the discussions were made possible by grants received from the United States Information Agency, the Embassy of Saudi Arabia, and Saudi-Aramco, to which we offer our thanks. Following the Anniversary, the participants visited Harvard University, Hartford Seminary, the University of Massachusetts, the University of Michigan, and U.C.L.A., where they gave speeches, met with faculty and students, and exchanged ideas with them. Recognition should also be given to the International Law Institute, first for serving as the home of the Society, and secondly for playing an important role in the Anniversary celebrations.

The views expressed in these papers are those of the individual authors.

GERALD E. LAMPE
Editor & Secretary for the Society

History of
The Shaybani Society of International Law

Majid Khadduri

The Shaybani Society was established in Europe in 1955. It was established to honor the great Hanafi jurist Muhammad Bin al-Hasan al-Shaybani (750 - 804) who wrote many works on the law governing the relationship of Islam with other countries called the *Siyar*. True, he was not the first to write on the subject, but he wrote extensively, and he was the first to consolidate all the legal material on the field, and to provide perhaps the most complete and thorough study of it. Not all of his works have yet seen the light.

A Turkish edition of Shaybani's work titled *al-Siyar al-Kabir,* with a commentary by Sarakhsi (d. 1101), was translated and published in Istanbul in 1825, which became a textbook on the subject. Joseph Hammer von Purgstall reviewed the book in the *Jahrbücher der Literatur*[1] and called Shaybani "the Hugo Grotius of the Muslims." "However surprising," wrote Hans Kruse, "the bestowal of such a title of honour on a Muslim jurist...by so great a scholar as Purgstall may have been, it did not find an echo among European scholars." Hans Kruse made another attempt to "secure for al-Shaybani that place in the history of International Law which he rightfully deserves given his importance,"[2] and he, in cooperation with other scholars, founded the Shaybani Society of International Law in 1955.

The initial steps taken to establish the Shaybani Society were made by correspondence. 'Abd al-Hamid Badawi, a distinguished Egyptian jurist and a Judge at the International Court of Justice, was elected President of the Society.[3] Salah al-Din al-Munajjid and I were elected Vice-Presidents. Hans Kruse acted as Secretary of the Society. Kruse, then Professor at Göttengen University (later at Böchum University), proved to be not only the spiritual father of

---

1. Wein, 1927, Vol. 40, p. 48.
2. Hans Kruse, "*The Foundation of Islamic International Jurisprudence*", Journal of the Pakistan Historical Society, Vol. III (1955), p. 238.
3. For a brief account of the life of Badawi, who died in 1965, *see* M. Khadduri, "*'Abd al-Hamid Badawi*", in W.F. Kuehl, ed., *Biographical Dictionary of Internationalists* (Westport and London, 1983), pp. 45-46.

the Society but also the central and most active figure in it. One of the scholars who cooperated with Kruse in the establishment of the Society was Muhammad Hamidullah of Hyderabad, who lived in Paris ever since his homeland was annexed by India after independence.

The purpose of the Society was not only to honor Shaybani as a great jurist, but also to publish his manuscripts, most of which are now scattered in various parts of the Islamic World. Al-Munajjid, then Director of the Arabic Manuscript Department at the Arab League in Cairo, was able to discover a number of unpublished manuscripts, and he edited and published Shaybani's *Kitab al-Siyar al-Kabir*, consisting of his earlier work on *Siyar* and Sarakhsi's commentaries, in five volumes. But these commentaries amount virtually to a new book, as Sarakhsi failed to reproduce Shaybani's original text, to which access was denied him when he was in prison while he composed his book. The text of the old Siyar may well be regarded as lost. Fortunately, an important part of the *Kitab al-Asl* (also called *Kitab al-Mabsut*), one of Shaybani's early and most comprehensive works, is devoted to the subject. The part of the book on *Siyar* in this work is Shaybani's own exposition on the subject. In a visit to Istanbul, I was able to obtain a photocopy of the manuscript and, in an English translation and an introduction on Shaybani's life and ideas, a book entitled *The Islamic Law of Nations*, was published at the Johns Hopkins University Press in 1966.[4]

In 1965 Abd al-Hamid Badawi, Judge and Vice-President of the International Court of Justice, suddenly died. For almost four years, the Shaybani Society was without a President and seemed almost non-existent. Hans Kruse, although keen about the survival of the Society, has suffered heart problems ever since he went to Böchum. He took several leaves from the University, seeking recovery at several resorts in Germany, France and Spain. He was thus not in a condition to look after the Society. Nor were al-Munajjid or I in touch with Kruse to see as to what we could do about the Society.

In 1969, the Orientalist Society held its meetings at the University of Michigan. As I learned that Hans Kruse and Muhammad Hamidullah were planning to attend the meetings, I thought their visit to the United States might be a suitable occasion to discuss the future of the Shaybani Society with them. Since I was not planning to attend the Conference of the Orientalist Society, I invited them to dinner at my house in Washington after the conference was over. At dinner, the question about the future of the Shaybani Society was our main subject of discussion. Hans Kruse apologized for his inability to pay attention to the Shaybani Society. I raised the question as to whether we should allow the Society to die a natural death. Hans, at once replied: "Look, as Judge Badawi, President of the Society, had passed away, you as first Vice-President, can act as President and deal with its affairs." Hamidullah, in support of Kruse's opinion,

---

4. Majid Khadduri, ed., *The Islamic Law of Nations: Shaybani's Siyar* (Baltimore, 1966).

urged me to undertake the responsibility of the Society. In reply, I said I would be delighted to serve the Society in any capacity, but it would be very difficult to conduct its business as long as its President, the Vice-President, and the Secretary are located in different countries and far from each other. I, therefore, suggested that Washington ought to be the location of the Society and a meeting might be called to elect the principal administrative officers. Hans Kruse and Hamidullah seemed quite satisfied with my suggestion, and I promised to keep them informed about the steps to be undertaken for reorganizing the Society.

The first person I had approached for cooperation in the reestablishment of the Shaybani Society in Washington was Herbert Liebesny. Herbert, a specialist on Middle Eastern affairs in the State Department, was informed about the idea of reestablishing the Shaybani Society in Washington and about its purposes. Without hesitation, Herbert promised to cooperate as he and I had already edited a book on *Law in the Middle East* (1955), published under the auspices of the Middle East Institute in Washington. I also approached Raymond Hare, a former diplomat and President of the Middle East Institute, William Sands, Editor of the *Middle East Journal*, and several others in Washington who showed readiness to cooperate in the establishment of the Society.

In order to formalize the establishment of the Shaybani Society in Washington, a meeting of several persons interested in the purposes of the Society was held in which the steps to be taken for organizing it were discussed. I was confirmed as Acting President of the Society and a committee of three, composed of Herbert Liebesny, William Sands and myself, was commissioned to prepare a draft statute for the Society subject to ratification by those who had agreed to become the founding fathers of the Society. The question of permission from the authorities of the D.C. Government was not formally discussed, as it was taken for granted that the Society would be under the auspices of the Johns Hopkins School of Advanced International Studies (SAIS), since I was then a member of its faculty and Director of the Center for Middle East Studies.[5] The committee for the drafting of the statute prepared the draft within a few days. Liebesny and I, as members of the American Society of International Law, made use of the statute of this society in preparing the draft of the Shaybani statute and Bill Sands, an experienced editor, assisted in the final version of the statute, formally called the Constitution of the Shaybani Society of International Law.[6]

In the middle of January 1970, the members who formally established the Shaybani Society met to ratify its Constitution. Some questions and suggestions

---

5. Several Members of the SAIS faculty, including Francis O. Wilcox, then Dean, attended some of the Society's meetings and one of them, Stephen Schwebel, served as a member of the Executive Committee before he became a Judge of the International Court of Justice at the Hague.

6. For the text of the Constitution, see Appendix.

were made, but the draft was finally adopted and the principal officers of the Society were elected. I became President of the Society, Herbert Liebesny Vice-President and Jacqueline Rizik Secretary. Other members of the Executive Committee, in accordance with the Constitution, were appointed. It was decided that the first annual meeting would be held in the fall of 1970. The Executive Committee subsequently met and decided that the subject of discussion would be on the legal position of the Arab States in the Gulf and some of the Gulf legal problems.

The Shaybani Society held its first annual meeting at the Cosmos Club on Saturday, October 3, 1970. The precedent was set that the members would meet first at noon before they sit for lunch. As membership in the Society is small, the speaker (occasionally more than one) is formally introduced even before the luncheon was over. Speakers are not required to prepare written speeches, and the questions from the floor were often informally addressed to the speaker.

At the first meeting of the Society, three speakers: Quincy Wright, who spoke on the subject of the general legal position of the Arab Gulf States; Liebesny, Vice-President of the Shaybani Society, spoke on some of the legal problems of the Gulf since World War II, and Rouhollah Ramazani, Professor at the University of Virginia, discussed a specific subject: the *Shatt al-Arab* frontier dispute between Iraq and Iran. During the discussion, it was felt that there were several other pending issues that were not touched upon, like the Buraymi dispute between Saudi Arabia and Abu Dhabi. For this reason, it was suggested that the Buraymi and other Gulf problems might be discussed in another meeting of the Society.

Following the first meeting, the Society held at least one annual meeting, but not infrequently, further meetings were held whenever an important issue was considered of interest to members of the Society. It is, however, not our purpose in this short account of the Society to provide a complete list of all the names of the speakers who addressed the Society. Perhaps it might be of interest to mention only some of the subjects and the distinguished men in official or unofficial capacities who addressed the Society.

In the second annual meeting of the Society in 1971, George Rentz, head of the Research Department at the Arab-American Oil Company (ARAMCO), discussed in detail the Saudi-Abu Dhabi dispute over the province of Buraymi, which had become a serious issue between the two countries and was submitted to arbitration for settlement by Saudi Arabia in 1955. Rens gave a detailed account of the dispute, but he hesitated to prepare a paper on the subject, perhaps mainly because he was involved in the preparation of a "Memorial" for ARAMCO in which the Saudi position on the dispute was presented.[7] As neither Rens nor the speakers on the legal position of the Gulf were enthusiastic

---

7. *See Memorial of the Government of Saudi Arabia* (Cairo, 1955) 3 vols., prepared by ARAMCO for the Saudi Arabian Government. The British Foreign Office Prepared a memorial for the Abu-Dhabi Government.

about the preparation of papers for publication, some members of the Shaybani Society felt that perhaps the speakers at the Society's meetings would speak more frankly on some sensitive issues if they were not obliged to prepare written speeches. It became a tradition of the Society that speakers were free to talk in any way they wanted. Some had actually prepared written speeches, but most of them preferred to use notes.

In most of the meetings of the Executive Committee, reflecting the feelings of other members of the Society, the subjects chosen for discussion were on the whole related to current issues in the Middle East. Before World War II, American interest in Islamic and Middle Eastern affairs was very limited, largely confined to academic studies of the ancient Near East and to missionary activities. But during and after World War II, in which the United States became increasingly more involved than ever before, the American public and academic institutions began to pay greater attention to Middle Eastern languages, and the socio-political and economic problems of the area. American business enterprises, particularly the oil (petroleum) companies, became increasingly more interested in Middle Eastern markets and resources, especially their oil. Thus, when the seat of the Shaybani Society was transferred from Europe to the United States, it was natural that a greater attention was paid to contemporary problems than to classical subjects.

The following list below does not include all the names of the speakers and subjects for discussion. It is rather intended to give an idea about how wide was the range of subjects selected for discussion by some of the most competent men in official and unofficial capacities whom the Society had sought to engage in its programs. The names of the speakers are as follows:

1. Quincy Wright, Liebesny, Ramazani, and George Rentz, as noted earlier, discussed the legal position and problems of the Persian (later called Arab) Gulf in the first and second annual meetings in the fall of 1970 and 1971.
2. Inis L. Claude, Professor of International Organizations at the University of Virginia, discussed "The India-Pakistan Conflict in International Law," on March 13, 1972.
3. 'Abdul Latif al-Hamad, Director of the Kuwait Fund for Arab Economic Development, gave a speech on "Regional Economic Cooperation," on September 28, 1972. Maurice J. Williams, Deputy Administrator, A.I.D., Department of State, made comments on al-Hamad's speech.
4. Sir William Luce, the last British Political Resident in the Persian Gulf 1961-66, discussed the "Unity Experiments in the Middle East: The Union of the Arab Amirates, an example of Arab Unity," on September 29, 1973.
5. Leonard Meeker, Vice-President and Director of the Trans-Arabian Pipe-Line Company. As lawyer and the negotiator for the Trans-Ara-

bian Pipe-Line, he discussed the project and its significance in the oil industry in the Middle East, on October 12, 1974.
6. Lord Caradon, British representative to the United Nations (who worked on the preparation of the draft U.N. Resolution 242 concerning the Arab-Israeli conflict of 1967), discussed the steps taken for the drafting, the content, and significance of the U.N. Resolution 242, on October 1, 1977.
7. David Newsom, Under-Secretary of State, and Robert Owen, Legal Adviser, Department of State, discussed the question of "The American Hostages in Iran" on September 26, 1981.
8. Abd al-Amir al-Anbari, Ambassador of Iraq to the United States, discussed the "Recent Legal Developments in the Iraq-Iran Conflict," on November 21, 1987.
9. Talcott W. Seelye, American Ambassador to Lebanon, discussed "The Crisis in Lebanon," on October 21, 1987.
10. John A. Westberg and Shirin Entezari, practicing lawyers in Washington, D.C., and experts on the Iranian legal system, discussed the "Legal System in Iran Before and After the Revolution," on April 23, 1988.
11. Richard A. Falk, Professor of International Law at Princeton University, discussed "The International Legal Implications of the Palestinian Uprising," on October 22, 1988.
12. Muhammad al-Mashat, Ambassador of Iraq to the United States, discussed "The Kurdish Question and Its Regional and International Implications," on October 27, 1990. (The decision to invite the Iraqi Ambassador to speak was made before Iraq had invaded Kuwait, but when the Shaybani Society was scheduled to meet after Iraq had invaded Kuwait, the Dean of the School of Advanced International Studies informed the Society that it would have to meet outside SAIS).
13. Robert Rosenstock, Counselor of Legal Affairs for the American Mission to the United Nations, discussed the subject of the Security Council's Resolutions concerning Iraq, on March 6, 1992.
14. Stephen C. McCaffrey, Professor of Law at McGeorge School of Law, The University of the Pacific, Sacramento, California, discussed the question of the distribution of water in the Middle East, on September 2, 1992.
15. Sadiq al-Azm, Professor at the University of Damascus, discussed the impact and significance of "Rushdi's *Satanic Verses*," on May 7, 1993.
16. Muhsin A. Al-Aini, Ambassador of Yaman to the United Nations, discussed "The Structure of the New Yaman," on October 15, 1993.
17. John Quigley, Professor at Ohio State University, discussed "The Legal Implications of the Oslo Palestine Accord," on October 13, 1995.
18. Shibley Telhami, Professor at Brown University, discussed "The Oslo Accords: Does Informed Diplomacy Matter?", on October 20, 1995.

In October 1990 the Society severed its affiliation with the School of Advanced International Studies and entered into an association with the International Law Institute.[8] Professor Don Wallace, Jr., Chairman of the Board of the Institute, also serves as vice-president of the Shaybani Society.

Ever since the Shaybani Society has been associated with the International Law Institute, an increasing number of meetings have been held partly owing to the fact that a series of crises have ensued in the wake of the Gulf War but mainly due to the Palestinian uprising which prompted the Shaybani Society to discuss some of the legal aspects of that issue. The Society was prompted to hold those meetings owing to the services and facilities offered by the Institute which were encouraging to increase its meetings. The Institute, finding that some of the persons who attended its own seminars seem to have shown an interest in attending some of the meetings of the Shaybani Society, have encouraged the Society to increase its meetings. Perhaps there was no better evidence for this trend than the cooperation shown during the celebration of the silver anniversary of the Shaybani Society in the fall of 1995.

The idea of celebrating the silver anniversary of the Shaybani Society was at first broached at a meeting of the Executive Committee early in 1994. The purpose of the celebration was not only to honor Shaybani, whose name the Society bears, but also to call the attention of both the members and friends of the Society that a quarter of a century had passed since the Society's headquarters had not merely been moved from one country to another, but that it had, indeed, been reborn as a new society in Washington.

But there was another purpose for celebrating the Society's silver anniversary. Ever since it was reestablished in Washington, almost all of the topics that have been discussed at the Society's meetings were either strictly legal or political. Only one topic, discussed by Professor Adda Bozeman, was about International Law from a cultural viewpoint. It was suggested that on the occasion of celebrating the twenty-fifth anniversary, perhaps a number of scholars from the Islamic World should be invited to participate in the celebration and to speak on such subjects as justice and human rights from the point of view of Islamic law.

Invitations to several Muslim scholars were sent and ten replied that they were ready to participate in the Shaybani Society's silver anniversary. The Shaybani Society held its meetings on October 27 and 28, 1995, in which the concepts of justice, Islamic and Western, were discussed. The text of the pa-

---

8. The severance arose out of a misunderstanding between Dean George R. Packard and the Society regarding an invitation to the Iraqi ambassador to deliver an address to the Shaybani Society on the SAIS premises after the invasion of Kuwait by Iraq. Although the proposed lecture was on a topic unrelated to the invasion, Dean Packard conveyed to the Society his view that the meeting was not in the interests of SAIS, a position that many in the Society viewed as a denial of essential academic freedom.

pers that were prepared for the anniversary are to be found in this Memorial volume of the Shaybani Society's silver anniversary.

As the U.S. Information Agency had shown an interest in inviting almost a dozen distinguished scholars from the Islamic World, it was arranged that this group would visit a number of academic institutions in New England, the Mid-West and the western coast of the United States. Thus, they were able to visit over half a dozen academic institutions where such subjects as freedom and human rights in the Islamic World were discussed with students and faculty.

Justice and Human Rights in Islam

Muhammad Tal'at Al-Ghunaimi[1]

INTRODUCTION

Justice is a complicated concept because it comprises various characteristics. It is referred to in the *Qur'an* under equivalent terms such as *adl* (fairness), *qist* (equity), *mizan* (balance), and *haqq* (right). It is, therefore, quite difficult to give a precise definition for justice. Perhaps this is a reason why one rarely could come across a standard definition in the classical teachings of Islam. The following definitions are examples of the attempts made by jurists to establish a general conception of justice in Islam.

Ibn Al-Rabi' views justice as the correctness of all actions, based on a harmony of the mental faculty and the animal nature in man. According to this view, justice is the highest function of government, and while no one doubts the need for its efficacy, there are differing views of its attainment which, nevertheless, reveal certain key points of agreement about its goals. Broadly stated, it involves placing everything in its proper place and giving everyone his due. Justice entails a threefold set of rights – rights due to God, rights due to the living, and rights due to the dead.

Among the rights due to the living are the repayment of debt, duties arising out of contractual relations, veracity in testimony, and certain ethical duties. The ruler is equally bound to do what is just, and justice in his case consists of keeping promises, being merciful, and giving everyone his share according to the law.

Objectivity and independence are among the qualities deemed necessary for a judge in the modern world, but despite our idealized conception of the judiciary, judges sometimes lack the integrity and independence which ought to be their chief merit, and we are forced to conclude that something is lacking

---

1. Professor of International Law, Alexandria University, Alexandria, Egypt.

in the standards set for judges were they to go astray. By comparison, Ibn Al-Rabi' set standards more than a thousand years ago which were of a very high order indeed.

Ibn Al-Rabi' states:

1. a judge should be God-fearing and dignified in demeanor;
2. he should have sound common-sense and be conversant with the best of judicial literature;
3. he should bear an absolutely impeccable character;
4. he should not deliver judgments before he is satisfied that full proof has been laid before him, nor delay judgment when sufficient evidence has been produced;
5. he should be fearless in awarding what is right and due;
6. he should accept no present nor hear any recommendations;
7. he should see no party concerned in private;
8. he should rarely smile, and speak little;
9. he should accept no favor from any party concerned;
10. he should take great care to protect the property of orphans.

A second perspective is provided by Muhammad Ibn Ka'b of Cordoba in response to a question from the *Caliph* 'Umar II (d. 720) for the definition of justice. In his reply, Ka'b stated that real justice was to deal with inferiors like a father, with a superior like a son, and with equals like a brother; and to award punishment only according to the wrong done and the power to bear it. He quotes 'Ali, the fourth *Caliph*, that the best judge is one who is not prejudiced in his decisions by personal desires, nor by leanings towards any such relationships. He should neither fear nor hope, but take a natural attitude towards all that comes before him.

It is in this sense of strict justice which prompted Abu Hamid al-Ghazzali (d. 504/1111) to insist on the absolute neutrality of the *Amir* (ruler) in all his acts or words. According to Ghazzali, the Amir should pay equal regard to all people, whether high or low, noble or downtrodden, and should put down lawlessness with a stern hand. He relates how someone once asked the great Sassanian minister, Buzurchimihr, which kings were the greatest, to which Buzurchimihr replied that the greatest were those who had the confidence of the good and were the terror of the wicked. He also relates the story of Alexander the Great, who asked the learned men how he could better his lot, to which they replied that he should eradicate both undue likings and undesirable prejudices, that he should not make any decision hurriedly without counsel and should shun all personal prejudices, at the time of sitting in judgment over other people.

Al-Ghazzali wrote a book, entitled *Tibru'l-Masbuk*, consisting of admonitions to the *Amir*. He sets out the qualities necessary for an ideal ruler – intellect, knowledge, proportionality, chivalry, love for his subjects, diplomacy, foresight, strength of will, and knowledge of current events and the history of his predecessors. Such an ideal ruler should also ensure that his magistrates, secretaries, viceroys and other officers did their work well. Ghazzali states that these are the fundamental qualities which make a ruler the shadow of God on earth. He relates how a learned man once told the *Caliph* Harun al-Rashid (d. 809) to remember that he was sitting where the first *Caliph* Abu Bakr (d. 634) once sat and was truthful; where 'Umar, the second *Caliph* once sat and differentiated between right and wrong; where *Caliph* 'Uthman (d. 656) once sat and was modest and bountiful; and where 'Ali, the fourth *Caliph*, once sat and was knowing and just. He also refers to Muhammad, the Apostle of Islam, who fed his cattle, tied his camel, swept his house, milked his goat, sewed his shoe, patched his clothes, ate with his servant, ground his corn in time of need, and bought his own food.

Ghazzali goes even so far as to lay down the daily routine of the ruler which might lead to his success in administration, giving detail of his food and drink, and the hours of privacy and desk work which he considers necessary for him. After morning prayers he should go out riding in order to investigate any wrong done to his subjects. He should then sit in court and allow everyone direct access to him so that he might have first hand knowledge of any complaints. He should make it a point of seeking the counsel of wise and experienced men and should make himself accessible to foreign envoys.

To summarize, justice is piety, taking care not to transgress limits ordained by God. "Do not exceed the limits of God, for those who exceed the bounds set by God are transgressors" (Q.II:229). It is noteworthy that Islam requires that believers should be just, even with their enemies. "O you who believe, stand up as witnesses for God in all fairness, and do not let the hatred of a people deviate you from justice. Be just: This is closest to piety; and beware of God. Surely God is aware of all you do" (Q.V:8). Justice is an all-embracing concept of the *Sharia'* which deals with almost all aspects of life, such as the following:

Personal Affairs: *Polygamy*

The practice of polygamy is limited by considerations of justice. For example, if a husband is unable to achieve justice between his wives, he is allowed to marry only one woman. Consequently, there is no polygamy in Islam. The *Qur'an* clearly states that "If you fear you cannot be equitable to orphan girls (in your charge, or misuse their persons), then marry women who are lawful for you, two, three, or four; but if you fear you cannot treat so many with equity, marry only one, or a maid or captive. This is better than being iniquitous" (Q.VI:3). Moreover, the *Qur'an* recognizes the difficulty of being equally just to two wives, stating that "Howsoever you may try, you will never be able to treat your wives equally. But do not incline (to one) exclusively and leave (the other) suspended (as it were). Yet if you do the right thing and are just, God is verily forgiving and kind" (Q.IV:129).

In Transactions: *The scribe should remember to act as if in the presence of God, with full justice to both parties.*

The art of writing should be seen as a gift from God. In an illiterate population the scribe has a higher ethical duty, both to the parties to the agreement as well as to the community as a whole. The *Qur'an* states that:

> O believers, when you negotiate a debt for a fixed term, draw up an agreement in writing, though better it would be to have a scribe write it faithfully down; and no scribe should refuse to write as God has taught him, and write what the borrower dictates, and have fear of God, his Lord, and not leave out a thing. If the borrower is deficient of mind or infirm, or unable to explain, let the guardian explain judiciously; and have two of your men to act as witnesses; but if two men are not available, then a man and two women you approve, so that in case one of them is confused, the other may remind her. When the witnesses are summoned they should not refuse (to come). But do not neglect to draw up a contract, big or small, with the time fixed for paying back the debt. This is more equitable in the eyes of God, and better as evidence for avoiding doubt. But if it is a deal about some merchandise requiring transaction face to face, there is no harm if no (contract is drawn up) in writing. Have witnesses to the deal, (and make sure) that the scribe or the witness is not harmed. If he is, it would surely be sinful on you part. And have fear of God, for God gives you knowledge, and God is aware of everything (Q.II:282).

In Court:

a. In giving testimony
An unbiased, truthful witness is necessary for the implementation of justice. The *Qur'an* states that "O you who believe, be custodians of justice (and) witnesses for God, even though against yourselves or your parents or relatives. Whether a man be rich or poor, God is his greater well-wisher than you. So follow not the behests of lust lest you swerve from justice; and if you prevaricate or avoid (giving evidence), God is cognizant of all that you do" (Q.IV:135).

b. In adjudication
The *Qur'an* admonishes judges to always consider justice when adjudi-

cating a case.

"God enjoins that you render to the owners what is held in trust with you, and that when you judge among the people, do so equitably. Noble are the counsels of God, and God hears all and sees everything" (Q.IV:58).

Justice and Human Rights

Justice is an abstract concept, which is better illustrated in the human rights context. A comparison of the Muslim conception of human rights and the Western approach therefore is instructive.

Individual human rights in the Western world are protected primarily by virtue of the following instruments:

- a: Universal Declaration of Human Rights;[2]
- b: Convention on the Prevention and Punishment of the Crime of Genocide;[3]
- c: International Covenant on Economic, Social and Cultural Rights;[4]
- d: International Covenant on Civil and Political Rights;[5] and the Optional Protocol to the International Covenant on Civil and Political Rights;[6]
- e: International Covenant on the Elimination of all Forms of Racial Discrimination[7] General Assembly Resolution 2106-B(XX) 19 January 1965:
- f: Some of the regional conventions concluded in implementation of the United Nations Declaration of Human Rights, such as the European Convention, the African Convention,[8] and the Universal Declaration of Human Rights promulgated by the Islamic Council on 19th, September 1981.

In fact, human rights and fundamental freedoms are considered part of natural law. "The pressure of necessity stimulates the impact of natural law

---

2. Universal Declaration of Human Rights, G.A. Res. 217A(III), U.N. Doc. A/810, at 71 (1948).

3. Convention on the Prevention and Punishment of the Crime of Genocide, Dec. 9, 1948, 78 U.N.T.S. 1021.

4. International Covenant on Economic, Social and Cultural Rights, G.A. Res. 2200A (XXI), 21 U.N. GAOR, Supp. No. 16, at 49, U.N. Doc. A/6316, 993 U.N.T.S. 14531 (1976).

5. International Covenant on Civil and Political Rights, 999 U.N.T.S. 14668 (1976).

6. Optional Protocol to the International Covenant on Civil and Political Rights, 999 U.N.T.S. 14668 (1976).

7. International Covenant on the Elimination of all Forms of Racial Discrimination, 660 U.N.T.S. 195.

8. African [Banjul] Charter on Human and People's Rights, June 27, 1981, OAU Doc. CAB/LEG/67/3 rev. 5.

and of moral ideas," said Lord Wright, which "convert[s] them into rules of law deliberately and overtly recognized by the consensus of civilized [nations]."[9]

Human rights may be viewed conceptually as either individual rights or collective rights. In the Western model, human rights concepts, as defined in the relevant international conventions are intended to benefit only the States party to that instrument, whereas in the Islamic model, the benefit of human rights protections extend to all humankind. In both concepts, for every right there is a corresponding duty, and in the concept of human rights, the duties fall upon the State. It follows that duties are the outgrowth of rights, and the fact that human rights are owed to the individual by the State as well as that "human duties" are owed by the individual to the State. But the State has always had other means at its disposal to ensure that duties are fulfilled. The whole movement for the protection of human rights arose as an attempt to redress the balance between the power of the State to impose duties on individuals and the powerlessness of the individual to ensure a correlative respect for his rights.

The American Declaration on the Rights and Duties of Man,[10] adopted in 1948, consists of ten articles setting out the duties of man, including the duty to support, educate and protect his minor children; to acquire at least an elementary education; to vote; to obey the law; to pay taxes; and to work.

The Universal Declaration of Human Rights states that "Everyone has duties to the community in which alone the full and free development of his personality is possible." Subsequent statements and conventions on human rights contain the stipulation that all States, bodies and persons have the duty to abstain from any act which abrogates any recognized human right.

International protection is achieved whenever the State is made responsible to some international body or authority for the implementation of its obligations in the field of human rights. Consequently, the distinctions between civil and political rights, and economic, social and cultural rights becomes important, because measures appropriate to the protection of each are quite distinct.

HUMAN RIGHTS IN ISLAM[11]

(1) The Physical Freedoms (Self and Body)

In comparison with the treatment of physical freedoms in the international

---

9. Lord Wright, *War Crimes Under International Law*, 62 L.Q.R.__, 51 (1946).
10. American Declaration on the Rights and Duties of Man, May 2, 1948.
11. For the text of the Muslim Universal Declaration on Human Rights, see the appendix attached to this article.

instruments on human rights, Islam recognizes the sayings of the Prophet that "all of the Muslims are forbidden to the other Muslim: his integrity, property and blood" and that "The Muslim is the man whom people are safe from his hand and his blackened tongue." Similarly, the *Qur'an* mandates the protection of human life by stating: "That is why We decreed for the children of Israel that whosoever kills a human being except (as punishment) for murder or for spreading corruption in the land, it shall be like killing all humanity" (Q.V:32), as well as the verse "Any one who kills a believer intentionally will be cast into Hell to abide there forever, and suffer God's anger and damnation. For him a greater punishment awaits" (Q.IV:93).

There is a certain societal value, recognized by Islam, in allowing a victim to retaliate against the wrongdoer. "In retribution there is life (and preservation). O men of sense, you may happily take heed for yourselves" (Q.II:179). Islam also prescribed immigration for those who are persecuted and cannot defend themselves. In fact, immigration in such case is both a right and an obligation. "As for those whose souls are taken by the angels (at death) while in a state of unbelief, they will be asked by the angels: 'What (state) were you in?' They will answer: 'We were oppressed in the land.' And the angels will say: 'Was not God's earth large enough for you to migrate?' Their abode will be Hell, and what an evil destination!" (Q.IV:97).

If immigration in the case of oppression is a right of the oppressed, it also gives rise to a duty for those who are able to assist such refugees. "Those who came to the city and to faith before them, love those who have taken refuge with them, and do not feel for themselves any need for what is given them, and give them preference over themselves even if they are indigent" (Q.LIX:9).

For the same rationale, Islam adopted the practice of providing *"jiwar" (self-protection)* to those who seek it, even if they are not Muslims. "If an idolater seeks protection, then give him asylum that he may hear the word of God. Then escort him to a place of safety, for they are people who do not know" (Q.IX:6).

Freedom from Want

Islam exhorts the Islamic State to provide at least the minimum required for a man to keep respectable, rather than to merely exist. This is the reason why a part of the *zakat* is paid for contingent debts, while another is designated for the poor and the needy. The Prophet says that "any group among whom someone spends the night hungry is deprived of God's *dhimma* and his Prophet's." Moreover the *Qur'an* emphasizes that "Piety lies in...disbursing your wealth out of love for God among your kin and the orphans, the wayfarers and mendicants..."(Q.II:177). Indeed, the act of providing for those less able is seen as a duty toward God. "And feed the needy for the love of Him, and the orphans and the captives, (Saying): 'We feed you for the sake of God, desiring neither recompense nor thanks" (Q.LIIVI:8-9).

Islam is concerned with the health of the individual and urges Muslims to be clean to the extent that cleanliness is considered one of the fundamental characteristics of believers. The Prophet condemns gluttony and advises believers to care for their health. Muslims are required to keep healthy and active and to offer help to the sick.

Islam also encourages marriage to the extent that the Islamic State, under the *Ummayed Caliph* 'Umar Bin 'Abd al-'Aziz (d. 720), used to pay the dowry for those who could not afford it. The Islamic view of linking the family with social development may be based on the *Qur'anic* verse "O Lord, give us comfort in our spouses and children, and make us paragons of those who follow the straight path" (Q.IIV:74). Umar used to pay an allowance for the children of needy families. This act might be considered a precedent for the modern system of social security.[12]

Islamic philosophy is quite concerned about the condition of orphans and considers any harm done to them as a crime. "Give to the orphans their possessions, and do not replace things of your own which are bad with things which are good among theirs, and do not intermix their goods with your own and make use of them, for this is a grievous crime" (Q.IV:2).

The Right to Work

Labor is both a right and an obligation of the Islamic community – man should not be a burden on society. The Prophet considered work to support one's self or needy parents as a *jihad*. The *Qur'an* says that "(Give to) the needy" (Q.II:273) and further admonishes "O believers, you should not usurp unjustly the wealth of each other...and do not destroy yourselves" (Q.IV:29).

The State is required to make available the opportunities for everyone who has the ability to work and to guarantee his rights. It is reported that the Prophet once gave two *dirhams* to a man and advised him to buy food with one *dirham* and buy an axe with the other to use as a tool for work. Al-Ghazzali said that the State should provide the needy with tools and equipment necessary for work. The *Qur'an* condemns those who abuse workers: "there was a king after them who used to seize every ship by force" (Q.XVIII:79). Moreover, the *Qur'an* tells believers not to "keep back from people what is theirs, and do not corrupt the land after it has been reformed" (Q.VII:85).

The *Caliph* 'Umar was keen to pay all of his agents salaries which were sufficient to live up to their responsibilities. The *Muhtasib* (public controller) used to supervise the labor market and make sure that women and children

---

12. Al Baladhuri, *Futuh Al Buldan* (Radwan Muhammad Radwan ed. 1959), pp. 438, 445.

were not abused. Islam guarantees the rights to work, as the *Qur'an* states: "Men have a share in what they earn, and women have theirs in what they earn" (Q.IV:32).

Nor were human rights and security neglected for non-Muslims, as such rights were acknowledged in the agreements concluded between the Prophet and the "Peoples of the Book" (Christians and Jews), who possessed their own revealed scriptures.[13]

Just Laws

All people tend to seek a just society where no innocent is punished and no criminal is released.[14] "We have surely sent apostles with clear signs, and sent with them the Book and the Balance, so that men may stand by justice...."(Q.LVII:25). The pursuit of justice was seen as a sacred obligation under the *Qur'an*. "God enjoins that you render to the owners what is held in trust with you, and that when you judge among the people do so equitably" (Q.IV:58). It is reported that *Caliph* 'Umar issued a declaration stating that his agents were not nominated to torture them or to do them injustice and he urged those who suffer from ill-treatment to submit a complaint to him. 'Amr Bin al-'As, the viceroy of Egypt, replied to the question as to "what if one of his people were subjected to force, would you retaliate for him?" 'Umar answered: "By Allah I do because I have seen the Prophet retaliating for himself."

Islam considers even the mere glance at the interior of a house to constitute in effect a breach of privacy, which the Prophet is reported to have admonished against. The Prophet also said "He who keeps the company of a grieved person until he proves his right shall find his feet steady on the day when feet are shaking." For example, the people of Samarqand complained to *Caliph* 'Umar Ibn 'Abd ul-'Aziz that the Muslim army entered their city without prior warning. 'Umar appointed a judge who found that their complaint was valid. Consequently, 'Umar ordered the army to leave the city. Impressed by the *Caliph's* decision in their favor, they accepted Islam as their religion.[15]

Moral Freedoms

Freedom of thought and religion in the Islamic State is mandated by the *Qur'an:* "There is no compulsion in matters of faith" (Q.II:256). The use of

---

13. Mustafa Al-Siba'i, *Ishtiraqiyatul Islam* (Cairo), p. 136.
14. Note that consistent with Western jurisprudence, Islam recognizes the principle of the presumption of innocence.
15. Al Baladhuri, *supra* note 11, at 411.

force is tolerated only in two instances: as a warning to enemies, and to establish peace and order. The *Qur'an* states: "Are you going to compel the people to believe, except by God's dispensation?" (Q.X:99). It also states that "Surely the believers and the Jews, Nazareans (Christians) and the Sabians, whosoever believes in God and the Last Day, and whosoever does right, shall have his reward with his Lord and will neither have fear nor regret" (Q.II:62).

Allah exhorts people to think and contemplate their surroundings. The *Qur'an* states: "Verily there are signs in this for those who reflect" (Q.XLV:13). The attitude of *Caliph* 'Ali towards the Khawarij is a case in point for the tolerance of the ruler. However, Islam does not tolerate apostasy, as the adoption of Islam is not imposed by force, consequently the subsequent renunciation of Islam is inconceivable. Such acts of apostasy are seen by some as high treason worthy of capital punishment.

Freedom of Association

Freedom of association is a logical extension of the freedom of the individual. This freedom was first expressed by the Khawarij during the time of *Caliph* 'Ali, who tolerated their existence so long as it was peaceful. It was brought to the attention of *Caliph* 'Umar Ibn 'Abd al-'Aziz that an opposition group named *"Harrouriyat Al Mawsil"* wished to dwell in a certain area. 'Umar answered that they were free to do whatever they wish so long as they did not hurt anybody, whether Muslim or non-Muslim.

Minority Rights: The concept of dhimma

The concept of *"dhimma"* is implied in the agreements reached between the Muslim authorities and non-Muslims of the conquered countries in which their rights and obligations were defined. These people were referred to as the *"dhimmis"*. In Spain the term *dhimma* was given to the Sephardic Jews, while Christians were called *"mu'ahid"*.[16]

The *dhimma* covenant had its origins in the concept of *jihad* which, in the classical sense, divides the world into two spheres: the abode of Islam and the abode of war. According to this doctrine, the abode of war along with all its inhabitants and property are destined to belong to the Muslims, or as the Latin maxim says *"Qucee ab hostibus capiuntur Statin capientive fiunt."*[17] In case the abode of war, or part of it, comes under Muslim control, its fate depends on how the territory came under the control of Islam, whether by force or by

---

16. Provencal, *Histore De L'Espagne Musulmane* (Paris 1944), Vol. 1, p. 56.
17. Things taken from enemies immediately become the property of the conquerors.

capitulation. The act of conquest, therefore, presented Muslims with the problem of how to deal with the non-Muslims of the conquered territories. The system of *dhimma* provided the solution to the problem, which was essentially a legal rather than a religious concept. The *dhimmis*, consisting of Jews, Christians, and Sabians, apart from pagans, were permitted to keep their religions. The *Qur'an* states: "God will judge between those who believe and the Jews, the Sabians, Christians and the Magians and the idolaters, on the Day of Judgment" (Q.XXII:17)

INDIVIDUAL, COLLECTIVE, AND GROUP RIGHTS

It is useful to distinguish individual rights from collective rights, and individual and collective rights from group rights. Individual rights are inherent in man's existence. Collective rights are those which an individual acquires as a result of his living in a society, such as the right to marry, the freedom of association, the right to join a trade union, and the right to vote, *inter alia*. Group rights are those which do not exist in relation to the individual, but only in relation to the group, such as the rights of minority groups and the right of a people to self-determination. Whereas individual rights are basic, irrespective of the level of development of the state, collective rights may well take a lower priority in less-developed states if it is thought that the rapid achievement of individual rights requires a strong government.

Before there can be any question of group rights, a group must be shown to exist. While objective criteria exist to demonstrate the existence of a minority group, the same does not always apply in relation to a "people". This fact, plus the absence of anybody capable of deciding the question with authority, renders the existence of these rights somewhat tenuous.

RIGHT OF GROUPS IN ISLAM (SELF-DETERMINATION)

The most important of the group rights is the right of a "people" to become a State. Self-determination in the Islam has a strong religious connotation in the sense that self-determination is only permitted on a religious basis and is recognized under two circumstances. If exercised by an Islamic community, the *Qur'an* encourages those in the community to "lose not heart, nor be grieved, for you will surely prevail if you are believers" (Q.III:139). The *Qur'an* also provides that "Permission is granted to those (who take up arms) who fight because they were oppressed. God is certainly able to give help to those [w]ho were driven away from their homes for no other reason than they said 'Our Lord is God'" (Q.XXII:39-40). The issue of self-determination is more problematic if exercised by a nation of the Book under pagan control – because the "People of the Book" are not alike – some of them are "a section upright, who recite the scriptures in the hours of the night and bow in adoration and pray, and believe in God and the Last Day...." (Q.III:113), and some do not.

In both cases, Islam permits resorting to force in the exercise of self-determination. The *Qur'an* says in this respect "What has come upon you that you fight not in the cause of God and for the oppressed, men, women and children, who pray: 'Get us out of this city, O Lord, whose people are oppressors; so send us a friend by your will, and send us a helper'" (Q.IV:75).

But what position should an Islamic State take towards a nation of the Book in its struggle to exercise the right of self-determination against a pagan State? In my opinion, the Islamic State should lend its support to the nation of the Book in such a case, because such a nation is described in the *Qur'an*, as a nation upstanding (Q.III:113). Allah describes them as "among the upright and doers of good" (Q.III:114). These are "People of the Book" fighting leaders of unbelief, and Allah says, "fight these specimens of faithlessness, for surely their oaths have no sanctity" (Q.IX:12).

The legitimacy of self-determination is controversial in Western legal theory. Whereas, subject to these limits, it is considered a "right" in Islamic legal theory. Perhaps this difference is because the criteria used to distinguish between self-determination and secession are rather vague in the Western model. In the Islamic theory, this distinction is clear-cut. Any movement that is directed to enhance Islam or to consolidate the unity of the believers could be viewed as a legitimate exercise of self-determination. Hence, the secession of an Islamic group from a larger Islamic group is unacceptable under Islamic law, and may be classified as either apostasy or civil war[18]. Originally, this classification of illegitimacy referred to those who challenged the *Caliph* 'Ali after his acceptance of the decision of the arbitration that took place between him and Mu'awiyah. Later it was expanded to cover any group that challenge their legal government. If they remain within the State and conduct their challenge peacefully they are to be treated as an opposition party. But if they dominate a territory and create trouble for the Islamic State, they are to be considered rebels and if they resort to force, then their action is considered to be civil war. As the *Qur'an* states, "If two groups of believers come to fight one another, promote peace between them. Then, if one of them turns aggressive against the other, fight against the aggressive party till it returns to God's authority" (Q.XL:9).

Conclusion

The acts of the Prophet demonstrate that justice was more than a mere

---

18. *Ahl al- Baghy.*

theoretical concept — it was state practice in the history of Islam. As the *Qur'an* states, "We have sent down to you the Book containing the truth, in whose light you should judge among the people as God has shown you, and do not be a contender for deceivers" (Q.IV:105).

The Commentators explain this passage with reference to the case of Ta'ima Ibn Ubairaq. It was suspected that he had stolen a suit of armor, and when the trail was hot, he planted the stolen property into the house of a Jew, where it was found. The Jew denied the charge and accused Ta'ima, but the sympathies of the Muslim community were with Ta'ima because of his nominal profession of Islam. The case was brought before the Apostle, who acquitted the Jew according to the strict principle of justice, as "guided by God." Attempts were made to prejudice him and deceive him into using his authority to favor Ta'ima. The story illustrates that the Islamic concept of justice is to be applied impartially, and the obligation to be just should never be sacrificed.

We are grateful to God for guiding us here. Never would we have been guided, if God had not shown us the way (Q.VII:43)

APPENDIX

Muslim Universal Declaration on Human Rights

issued by The Islamic Council

PREAMBLE

Whereas the age-old human aspiration for a just world order wherein people could live, develop and prosper in an environment free from fear, oppression, exploitation and deprivation, remains largely unfulfilled;

Whereas the Divine Mercy unto mankind reflect in its having been endowed with super-abundant economic sustenance is being wanted, or unfairly or unjustly withheld from the inhabitants of the earth;

Whereas Allah has given mankind through His revelations in the Holy *Qur'an* and the *Sunnah* His of His Blessed prophet Mohammad and abiding legal and moral framework within which to establish and regulate human institution and relationship;

Whereas the human rights decreed by the Divine law aim at conferring dignity and honour on mankind and are designed to eliminate oppression and injustice;

Whereas by virtue of their Divine source and sanction these rights can neither be curtailed, abrogated nor disregarded by authorities, assemblies or other institutions, nor can they be surrendered or alienated;

Therefore we, as Muslims, who believe

a. in God, the Benificent and Merciful, the Creator, Sustainer, the Sovereign, the sole Guide of mankind and the Source of all law;
b. in the Viceregency (*Khilafah*) of man who has been created to fulfil the Will of God on earth;
c. in the wisdom of divine guidance brought by the Prophets, whose mission found its culmination in the final Divine message that was conveyed by the Prophet Mohammad (Peace be unto him) to all mankind;
d. that rationality be itself without the light of revelation from God can neither be a sure guide in the affairs of mankind nor provide spiritual nourishment to the human soul, and knowing that the teachings of Islam represent the quintessence of Divine guidance in its final and perfect form, feel duty-bound to remind man of the high status and dignity bestowed on him by God;

Justice and Human Rights in Islam • 15

e. in inviting all mankind to the message of Islam;
f. that by the terms of our primeval covenant with God, our duties and obligations have priority over our rights, and that each of us is under a bounded duty to spread the teachings of Islam by word, deed, and indeed in all gentle ways, and to make them effective not only in our individual lives but also in the society around us;
g. in our obligation to establish an Islamic order;
   i. wherein all human beings shall be equal and none shall enjoy a privilege or suffer a disadvantage or discrimination by reason of race, colour, sex, origin, or language;
   ii. wherein all human beings are born free;
   iii. wherein slavery and forced labour are abhorred;
   iv. wherein conditions shall be established such that the institution of family shall be preserved, protected and honoured as the basis of all social life;
   v. wherein the rulers and the ruled alike are subject to, and equal before, the Law;
   vi. wherein obedience shall be rendered only to those commands that are in consonance with the Law;
   vii. wherein all worldly power shall be considered as a sacred trust, to be exercised within the limits prescribed by the Law and in a manner approved by it, and with due regard for the priorities fixed by it;
   viii. wherein all economic resources shall be treated as Divine blessings bestowed upon mankind, to be enjoyed by all in accordance with the rules and the values set out in the *Qur'an* and the *Sunnah*;
   ix. wherein all public affairs shall be determined and conducted, and the authority to administer them shall be exercised after mutual consultation (*Shura*) between the believers qualified to contribute to a decision which would accord well with the Law and the public good;
   x. wherein everyone shall undertake obligations proportionate to his capacity and shall be held responsible *pro rata* for his deeds;
   xi. wherein everyone shall, in the case of an infringement of his rights, be assured of appropriate remedial measures in accordance with the Law;
   xii. wherein no one shall be deprived of the rights assured to him by the Law except by its authority and to the extent permitted by it;
   xii. wherein every individual shall have the right to bring legal action against anyone who commits a crime against society as a whole or against any of its members;
   xiv. wherein every effort shall be made to

a. secure into mankind deliverance from every type of exploitation, injustice and oppression.
b. ensure to everyone security, dignity, and liberty in terms set out and by methods approved and within the limits set by the Law:

> *Do hereby, as servants of Allah and as members of the Universal Brotherhood of Islam, at the beginning of the Fifteenth century of the Islamic era, affirm our commitment to uphold the following inviolable and inalienable human rights that we consider are enjoined by Islam.*

I. Right to Life

a. Human life is sacred and inviolable and every effort shall be made to protect it. In particular no one shall be exposed to injury or death, except under the authority of the Law.
b. Just as in life, so also after death, the sanctity of a person's body shall be inviolable. It is the obligation of believers to see that a deceased person's body is handled with due solemnity.

II. Right to Freedom

a. Man is born free. No inroads shall be made on his right to liberty except under the authority and in due process of the Law.
b. Every individual and every people has the inalienable right to freedom in all its forms - physical, cultural, economic and political - and shall be entitled to struggle by all means against any infringement or abrogation of this right; and every oppressed individual or people has a legitimate claim to the support of other individuals and/or peoples in such a struggle.

III. Right to Equality and Prohibition Against Impermissible Discrimination

a. All persons are equal before the Law and are entitled to equal opportunities and protection of the Law.
b. All persons shall be entitled to equal wage for equal work.
c. No person shall be denied the opportunity to work or be discriminated against in any manner or exposed to greater physical risk by virtue of religious belief, colour, race, origin, sex, or language.

IV. Right to Justice

a. Every person has the right to be treated in accordance with the Law, and only in accordance with the Law.
b. Every person has not only the right but also the obligation to protest against injustice; to recourse to remedies provided by the Law in respect of any unwarranted personal injury or loss; to self-defence against any charges that are preferred against him and to obtain fair adjudication before an independent judicial tribunal in any dispute with public authorities or any other person.
c. It is the right and duty of every person to defend the rights of any other person and the community in general (*Hisba*).
d. No person shall be discriminated against while seeking to defend private and public rights.
e. It is the right and duty of every Muslim to refuse to obey any command which is contrary to the Law, no matter by whom it may be issued.

V. Right to Fair Trial

a. No person shall be adjudged guilty of an offence and made liable to punishment except after proof of his guilt before an independent juridical tribunal.
b. No person shall be adjudged guilty except after a fair trial and after reasonable opportunity for defence has been provided to him.
c. Punishment shall be awarded in accordance with the Law, in proportion to the seriousness of the offence and with due consideration of the circumstances under which it was committed.
d. No act shall be considered a crime unless it is stipulated as such in the clear wording of the Law.
e. Every individual is responsible for his actions. Responsibility for a crime can not be vicariously extended to other members of his family or group, who are not otherwise directly or indirectly involved in the commission of the crime in question.

VI. Right to Protection Against Abuse of Power

Every person has the right to protection against harassment by official agencies. He is not liable to account for himself except for mankind a defence to the charges made against him or where he is found in a situation wherein a question regarding suspicion of involvement in a crime could be reasonably raised.

VII. Right to Protection Against Torture

No person shall be subject to torture in mind or body, or degraded, or threatened with injury either to himself or to anyone related to or held dear by him, or forcibly made to confess to the commission of a crime, or forced to consent to an act which is injurious to his interests.

VIII. Right to Protection of Honour and Reputation

Every person has the right to protect his honour and reputation against calumnies, groundless charges or deliberate attempts at defamation and blackmail.

IX. Right to Asylum

   a. Every persecuted or oppressed person has the right to seek refuge and asylum. This right is guaranteed to every human being irrespective of race, religion, colour and sex.
   b. Al Masjid Al Haram (the sacred house of Allah) in Mecca is a sanctuary for all Muslims.

X. Rights of Minorities

   a. The *Qur'anic* principle "There is no compulsion in religion" shall govern the religious rights of non-Muslim minorities.
   b. In a Muslim country, religious minorities shall have the choice to be governed in respect of their civil and personal matters by Islamic Law or their own laws.

XI. Right and Obligation to Participate in the Conduct and Management of Public Affairs

   a. Subject to the Law, every individual in the community (*Umma*) is entitled to assume public office.
   b. Process of free consultation (*Shura*) is the basis of the administrative relationship between the government and the people. People also have the right to choose and remove their rulers in accordance with this principle.

XII. RIGHT OF FREEDOM OF BELIEF, THOUGHT AND SPEECH

a. Every person has the right to express his thoughts and beliefs so long as he remains within the limits prescribed by the Law. No one, however, is entitled to disseminate falsehood or to circulate reports which may outrage public decency, or to indulge in slander, innuendo, or to cast defamatory aspersions on other persons.
b. Pursuit of knowledge and the search for truth is not only a right but a duty of every Muslim.
c. It is the right and duty of every Muslim to protest and strive (within the limits set out by the Law) against oppression even if it involves challenging the highest authority in the State.
d. There shall be no bar on the dissemination of information provided it does not endanger the security of the society or the State and is confined within the limits imposed by the Law.
e. No one shall hold in contempt or ridicule the religious beliefs of others or incite public hostility against them; respect for the religious feelings of others is obligatory on all Muslims.

XIII. RIGHT TO FREEDOM OF RELIGION

Every person has the right to freedom of conscience and to worship in accordance with his religious beliefs.

XIV. RIGHT OF FREE ASSOCIATION

a. In their economic pursuits, all persons are entitled to the full benefits of nature and all its resources. These are blessings bestowed by God for the benefit of mankind as a whole.
b. All human beings are entitled to earn their living according to the Law.
c. Every person is entitled to own property, individually, or in association with others. State ownership of certain economic resources in the public interest is legitimate.
d. The poor shall have the right to a prescribed share in the wealth of the rich, as fixed by *Zakah*, levied, and collected in accordance with the Law.
e. All means of production shall be utilized in the interest of the community (*Umma*) as a whole, and may not be neglected or misused.
f. In order to promote the development of a balanced economy and to protect society from exploitation, Islamic law forbids monopolies, unreasonable restrictive trade practices, usury, the use of coercion

in the making of contracts and the publication of misleading advertisements.
g. All economic activities are permitted provided they are not detrimental to the interests of the community (*Umma*) and do not violate Islamic laws and values.

XVI. Right to Protection of Property

No property may be expropriated except in the public interest and no payment of fair and adequate compensation.

XVII. Status and Dignity of Workers

Islam honours work and the worker and enjoins Muslims not only to treat the worker justly but also generously. He is not only to be paid his earned wages promptly, but is also entitled to adequate rest and leisure.

XVIII. Right to Social Security

Every person has the right to food, shelter, clothing, education, and medical care consistent with the resources of the community. This obligation of the community extends in particular to all individuals who cannot take care of themselves owing to some temporary or permanent disability.

XIX. Right to a Found a Family and Related Matters

a. Every person is entitled to marry, to found a family, and to bring up children in conformity with his religion, traditions and culture. Every spouse is entitled to such rights and privileges and carries such obligations as are stipulated by the Law.
b. Each of the partners in a marriage is entitled to respect and consideration from the other.
c. Every husband is obligated to maintain his wife and children according to his means.
d. Every child has the right to be maintained and brought up by its parents, it being forbidden that children are made to work at an early age or that any burden be put on them which would arrest or harm their natural development.
e. If parents are for some reasons unable to discharge their obligations

toward a child, it becomes the responsibility of the community to fulfil these obligations at public expense.
f. Every person is entitled to material support, as well as care and protection, from his family during his childhood, old age, or incapacity. Parents are entitled to material support as well as care and protection from their children.
g. Motherhood is entitled to special respect, care, and assistance on the party of the family and the public organs of the community (*Ummah*).
h. Within the family, men and women are to share in their obligations and responsibilities according to their sex, their natural endowments, talents, and inclinations, bearing in mind their common responsibilities toward their progeny and their relatives.
i. No person may be married against his or her will, or loss or suffer diminution of his legal personality on account of marriage.

XX. RIGHT OF MARRIED WOMEN

Every married women is entitled to:
a. live in the house in which her husband lives;
b. receive the means necessary for maintaining a standard of living which is not inferior to that of her spouse, and in the event of divorce, receive during the statutory period of waiting (*'Idda*) means of maintenance commensurate with her husband's resources, for herself as well as for the children she nurses or keeps, irrespective of her own financial status, earnings or property that she may hold in her own right;
c. seek and obtain dissolution of marriage (*Khul'a*) in accordance with the terms of the Law. This right is in addition to her right to seek divorce through the courts;
d. inherit from her husband, her parents, her children and other relatives according to the Law;
e. strict confidentiality from her spouse, or ex-spouse if divorced, with regard to any information that he may have obtained from her, the disclosure of which could prove detrimental to her interests. A similar responsibility rests upon her in respect of her spouse or ex-spouse.

XXI. RIGHT OF EDUCATION

a. Every person is entitled to receive education in accordance with his natural capabilities.
b. Every person is entitled to a free choice of profession and career and to the opportunity for the full development of his natural endowments.

XXII. Right of Privacy

Every person is entitled to the protection of his privacy.

XXIII. Right of Freedom of Movement and Residence

a. In view of the fact that the World of Islam is veritably *Umma Islamia*, every Muslim shall have the right to move freely in and out of any Muslim country.
b. No one shall be forced to leave the country of his residence, or be arbitrarily deported therefrom, without recourse to due process of law.

Explanatory Notes

1. In the above formulation of Human Rights, unless the context provides otherwise:
    a. the term "person" refers to both male and female sexes.
    b. the term "Law" denotes the *Shari'a*, i.e., the totality of ordinances derived from the *Qur'an* and the *Sunna* and any other laws that are deduced from the sources by methods considered valid in Islamic jurisprudence.
2. Each one of the Human Rights enunciated in this Declaration carries a corresponding duty.
3. In exercise and enjoyment of the rights referred to above, every person shall be subject only to such limitations as are enjoined by the law for the purpose of securing the due recognition of, and respect for, the rights and the freedoms of others and the general welfare of the Community (*Umma*).
4. The Arabic text of this Declaration is the original.

The Conception of Justice: Western and Islamic

Liaquat Ali Siddiqui[1]

INTRODUCTION

The conception of justice has been an issue of concern and interest of many disciplines including law, sociology, political science and philosophy. The theory of justice is interconnected with legal, political and philosophical theories.[2] What is justice, what are the criteria of determining justice, what is the relationship of justice to law, morality and right, how justice can be achieved, what are the different approaches to justice, and whether justice is relative or universal — these are the concerns and quests of the theory of justice.

Although the administration of justice is regarded as one of the most important functions of a state, the answer to the question how justice will be realized varies from state to state.

Both the West and Islam present their own approaches to the conception of justice. The Islamic model of justice has been practised for almost fifteen hundred years in different societies having linguistic, customary and cultural variations. Although Islam speaks of divine justice, it has within its system characteristics of equity, equality, humanity and also adaptability which have made Islamic justice acceptable and viable in different times and ages to different groups of people. Islam possesses a long experienced, well-tested and highly rich jurisprudence.

Western jurisprudence also has gone through different historical changes and developments and has been enriched by different streams of thought of different scholars and jurists.

From this perspective, a comparison between the Western and Islamic approaches to the conception of justice deserves merit. In this paper, Western and

---

1. Assistant Professor of Law, University of Dhaka, Bangladesh.
2. W. Friedmann, *Legal Theory* (5th ed., 1967), p. 3-4.

Islamic theories of justice will be first examined, then a comparison will be made between the two approaches, and lastly, some observations will be drawn.

WESTERN CONCEPTION OF JUSTICE

In this section an attempt will be made to examine the Western conception of justice as dealt with by the Western philosophers and jurists.

Plato and Aristotle, who belong to the idealistic philosophical school, deserve our first attention. Plato considers justice as a value concept. Plato's concept of justice has two aspects: Social Justice and Individual Justice. *Social Justice* represents a harmonious relation between various groups of society. It is achieved when each societal class performs its specified duties, allocated according to the nature of each class and the one does not intermeddle with the another. Thus, "Seeing then, I said, that there are three distinct classes, any meddling of one with another, or the change of one into another, is the greatest harm to the State, and may be most justly termed evil doing."[3] To Plato, virtue is justice. A perfect balance and equilibrium among the classes may give rise to such virtues. "This then is justice, and on the other hand when the trader, the auxiliary, and the guardian each does his own business, that is justice and will make the city just."[4]

Individual Justice, on the other hand, is achieved when one performs the acts for which one is best fitted by nature. A soldier who performs the duties of a philosopher king acts contrary to the nature of the soul and thereby creates chaos and turmoil in the society. According to Plato, individuals acting in conformity with their nature, achieve not only individual justice for themselves, but also social justice at the same time. Therefore, social justice is inconceivable without individual justice. Thus, Plato's conception of justice is based on the role of man without at the same time ignoring the role of society.

Aristotle's conception of justice is concerned more with the application of law and therefore marks a difference with the platonic conception of justice as complete virtue devoid of any reference to law. Aristotle suggests three kinds of justice (1) General or Universal justice (2) Particular justice and (3) Commutative justice.

General Justice is achieved by obedience to the laws of the land. *Particular Justice*, may be subdivided conceptually into two sub-categories: distributive justice and corrective, or remedial justice. The former is meted out by the legislator and consists of the distribution of offices, rights, honours and goods to the members of the community in accordance with the principle of propor-

---

3. Plato, *The Dialogues of Plato-The Republic*, tr. Jowett, (Random House 1937), Vol. 1, p. 697.
4. *Id.* at 698.

tionate equality. The latter guarantees, protects and maintains the distribution against illegal usurpation. Thus, corrective justice is designed to maintain the system which distributive justice has created. Corrective justice, administered by the judge, reestablishes the *status quo* by returning to the victim that which belonged to him or by compensating him for the loss. The third form of justice, *Commutative or Commercial Justice*, aims to regulate transactions and maintain fairness by equalizing the values of different products by a common standard of measurement.[5]

According to Ulpian (d. 228), a Roman jurist, justice is "the constant and perpetual will to render to everyone those things to which he is entitled." Cicero also described justice as "the disposition of the mind to render to every one his due." St. Thomas Aquinas defined justice as "a habit whereby a man renders to each one his due by a constant and perpetual will."[6] These definitions represent the so-called *Suum Cuique* (to each his due) formula of justice. The subjective elements in these definitions are based on universal character.

The conception of justice developed by the social contractualists is of different type. Both John Locke (d. 1704) and Rousseau (d. 1788) uphold the importance of natural laws and natural rights and put emphasis on obedience to such laws. Thomas Hobbes (d. 1679), on the other hand, treats positive or civil law as the most supreme rather than natural law. The conception of justice has also been conceptualized by them in relation to man's agreement to form a society through a pact.

Hobbes maintains that justice depends on positive law – that which is lawful is just, otherwise unjust. So the question of justice or injustice can be raised only when there is positive law. In the pre-social state of nature there was no positive law. Law comes into being only with the formation of the commonwealth, and justice is accomplished by the unconditional obedience to the Sovereign's dictates.[7] So justice to him is a product of social contract.

Unlike Hobbes, Locke considers justice not as a product of social contract, rather Locke's social contract presupposes the concept of justice. The ideas of just actions and unjust actions were very much there before men agreed to form society through a pact. He upholds the supremacy of justice over the State and Sovereign.

According to Emmanuel Kant (d. 1804), Law is the most just and moral form. To him, there is no unjust and immoral law. He holds that "reason" is infallible and the dictates of reason (the "categorical imperative") are most rational and therefore most moral and just. According to Kant, to act according to the dictate of reason is to act justly and to act according to instinct is to act

---

5. *See* Aristotle, *Nicomachean Ethics*, Book V.
6. Edgar Bodenheimer, *Jurisprudence: the Philosophy and Method of the Law* (1970), p. 184.
7. *See* Thomas Hobbes, *Leviathan*, Part 1, Ch.13.

unjustly. Given that infallible reason or categorical imperative represents the same source of both morality and law, Kant finds no contradiction between positive law and moral law, although laws operate in the external sphere and morality in the internal sphere. Thus, "Whatever is juridically in accordance with external laws, is said to be just and whatever is not juridically in accordance with external laws, is unjust."[8] According to Karl Mannheim, Kant places "all the moral emphasis not upon objective and overt behavior and its visible consequences, but upon the intention of the doer."[9]

The Utilitarians like Bentham (d. 1832), on the other hand consider justice from a different point of view. To them utility is the ultimate standard of morality and the conception of justice is related to the principle of utility. As an ethical theory, utilitarianism holds that the ultimate end is and ought to be general happiness and that an action is considered to be right and just if it brings the greatest happiness for the greatest number of people. Actions done either by individual human beings or by the State can be treated as just, virtuous, moral or legal if these bring general happiness. Actions are judged on the merit of their consequences.

Utilitarians with the aim of accelerating the social good sometimes undermine the natural rights and liberties of individuals. They even try to make all natural rights and liberties subservient to social good. Rights and duties are justified if the aim is only to achieve or try to achieve the social good. Bentham explains the principle of utility in the following way: "Nature has placed mankind under the governance of two sovereign masters, pain and pleasure. It is for them alone to point out what we ought to do, as well as to determine what we shall do. On the one hand, the chain of causes and effects, are fastened to their throne. They govern us in all we do, in all we say, in all we think…"[10]

Again representatives of the Positivist school of jurisprudence identify justice in isolation of law. John Austin (d. 1859) and Hans Kelsen (d. 1973) belong to this group. Austin defines a law as "a rule laid down for the guidance of an intelligent being by an intelligent being having power over him."[11] Law is thus strictly divorced from justice and instead of being based on ideas of good and bad, is based on the power of a superior. Hans Kelsen's pure theory of law is also an attempt to separate morality from law. According to him, "The task of legal theory is to clarify the relations between the fundamental and all lower norms, but not to say whether this fundamental norm

---

8. Emmanuel Kant, *The Philosophy of Law*, tr. W. Hastie, (Clifton, NJ, Augustus M. Kelly Pub. 1974), p. 32.
9. Karl Mannheim, *Diagnosis of Our Time* (New York, 1944), p.122.
10. Jeremy Bentham, *An Introduction to the Principle of Morals and Legislation and the Principles of Civil Codes*, in *The Works of Jeremy Bentham* (John Bowring ed. Edinburgh, 1843), Vol. 1, at Ch.1, 1.
11. Friedmann, *supra* note 1, at 258.

itself is good or bad. That is the task of political science, or of ethics or of religion."[12]

Friedmann has commented on the attitude of the Neo-Kantian philosophers toward the concept of justice:

> The different schools of Neo-Kantian philosophers have realized the relativity of justice and the dualism between eternal justice and positive law. They have, therefore, divorced the idea of justice from positive law. Some have refused to study the varying contents of the idea of justice as irrelevant to legal science (Vienna school), alternatively they have formulated the main conflicting ideals of justice (Radbruch) or attempted in vain to fill the formal idea of justice with a substantial content (Stammler). What emerges from all these varying attempts is the failure to establish absolute standards of justice except on a religious basis.[13]

Von Savigny (d. 1861), the most eminent exponent of the Historical School, holds that law, like language, is a product not of arbitrary and deliberate will but of slow, gradual, and organic growth. The true sources of law are popular faith, custom and the common consciousness of the people. Law is determined, like the language, the constitution, and the manners of the people, by the peculiar character of a nation, by its "national spirit" (*Volksgeist*). To Savigny, law is identical with the opinion of the people in matters of right and justice. Thus, the theories of Historical School came as a reaction against the natural law theories which did not consider the historical aspects of evolutionary processes.

Dean Roscoe Pound (d. 1964), the founder of American sociological jurisprudence, developed his theory of justice on the basis of Bentham's theory of utility. He considered the end of law principally in terms of maximum satisfaction of wants with least sacrifice. According to sociological jurisprudence, law is a social institution and should ensure that the making, interpretation, and application of laws take account of social facts. To him, the task of law is "social engineering" which represents a balance between the competing interests in society. As Pound noted, "For the present purpose I am content to see in legal history the record of a continually wider recognizing and satisfying of human wants or claims or desires through social control, a more embracing and more effective securing of social interests, a continually more complete and effective elimination of waste and precluding of friction in human enjoyment of the goods of existences in short, a continually more efficacious social engineering."[14] He suggests that justice may be administered with or without law. Justice administered according to law ensures equality and certainty and

---

12. *Id.* at 277.
13. *Id.* at 346.
14. Bodenheimer, *supra* note 5, at 110.

justice administered without law (according to the will or intuition of an individual decision-maker, but not on the basis of any fixed legal norm) helps solve new situations and problems for which law has laid down no rule. He argues that law must be stable and yet it cannot stand still. To Pound the first form of justice is judicial and the second administrative in character.

Jerome Frank (d. 1957) and Karl Llewellyn (d. 1962), who belong to the legal realist school of American jurisprudence, study law in its actual working. To them law is what judges decide and therefore, it is not proper to stick to the myth of legal certainty in the name of precedent or codification. This movement is a combination of both analytical positivist and sociological approaches. The ideal of justice is put to one side while investigating what the law is and how it works. Thus, the legal realists are interested in the aim and end of the law.

In the West, towards the end of the 19th and the beginning of 20th century, there has been a revival of natural law theories. The distinguished scholars of this trend include Stammler (d. 1938), John Rawls, Clarence Morris, Del Vecchio, L.L. Fuller, and H.L.A. Hart. Friedmann observes:

> As the faith of certainty wavers, idealistic philosophy revives, in the field of law this means once more a search for ideals of Justice...at least three widely different ways in which natural law re-entered the field ...the first leads straight back to the scholastic conception of natural law and is little more than a modernization of the catholic theory of law ... the second and third trends both show, as against the absolute ideals of schoolmen and rationalists, the skepticism of a world which feels that all values are relative and that no absolute ideal of justice can hope for universal recognition and validity.[15]

It appears that the conception of justice in the West has received different treatments in different times and ages by different scholars and jurists. The extreme naturalists viewed justice as an abstract, universal and moral ideal whereas, the extreme positivists viewed justice as an idea entirely irrelevant to the actual understanding of law in the working. And modern naturalists viewed justice in a new form which strives to take account, not only of knowledge contributed by the analytical, historical and sociological approaches, but also of the increasingly collectivist outlook on life. They explain justice as relative rather than universal, as changeable rather than unchangeable, and also as having concern for practical problems rather than abstract ideas.

ISLAMIC CONCEPTION OF JUSTICE

In Islam the word justice has its own meaning. The term justice is ex-

---

15. Friedmann, *supra* note 1, at 152-53.

pressed in such words as *adl, qist, mizan* as used in the *Qur'an*.[16] These terms are antonyms of *zulm* or injustice. Justice, in Islam, is given the highest status; for the Creator Allah has introduced Himself to be the most just arbitrator and justice to be His inseparable quality. One of the prime objectives of the Islamic mission is, as described in the *Qur'an*, to establish justice on earth. Thus, "We sent aforetime our apostles with clear signs and sent down with them the book and the balance (of right and wrong), that men may stand forth in justice (Q.L:25)."

The general approach of Islam is to judge the validity of any act or omission in the light of Islamic teachings. Islam does not consider an action to be just which goes against the basic principles of Islam. The guiding principle is whether the given act corresponds or contradicts Islamic teachings. Therefore, justice in Islam means acting in particular circumstances as prescribed by Islamic injunctions. Legally, it may mean settling the disputes between two opposite parties according to the Islamic injunctions.

Allah, the Almighty, is the supreme law-giver in Islam. He with His unlimited knowledge and wisdom, has directed us what to do in a particular situation. Therefore, His direction is bound to be just, although we do or do not realise the meaning and purpose of these directions by our limited knowledge. Absolute justice is known only to the Almighty, for He alone knows what is good for mankind. Hence, it is always safe to act as directed by Him. To know the objective good is beyond our power. Thus, "You may dislike a thing, yet it may be good for you; or a thing may happily please you but may be bad for you. Only God has knowledge, and you do not know"(Q.II:216). "[K]nowledge we have none except what You have given us, for you are all-knowing and all-wise" (Q.II:32).

The basis of administering justice in Islam are the Holy *Qur'an, sunna, ijma', qiyas*. Thus to quote the *Qur'an:* "We have sent down to you the Book containing the truth, in whose light you should judge among the people as God has shown you, and do not be a contender for deceivers"(Q.IV:105). God directed the Prophet in *Surat Al-An'am,* "Then should I seek (the source of) law elsewhere than God, when it is He who has revealed this Book to you, which distinctly explains (every thing)?"(Q.VI:114) "And to you We have revealed the Book containing the truth, confirming the earlier revelations, and preserving them (from change and corruption). So judge between them by what has been revealed by God…"(Q.V:48).

Taking any other basis for administering justice other than the guidance of Allah has been categorically rejected. The *Qur'an* states: "And those who do not judge in accordance with what God has revealed are transgressors"(Q.V:47) "[T]herefore, do not fear men, fear Me, and barter not My messages away for a paltry gain. Those who do not judge by God's revelations are infidels in-

---

16. 34 All Pakistan Legal Decisions 5 (1982).

deed" (Q.V:44). "And those who do not judge by God's revelations are unjust"(Q.V:45).

The demand for justice is so high and strict that one is expected to do justice even at the face of probable temptations — (1) favour to the nearest relatives, "Oh you who believe, be custodians of justice (and) witnesses for God, even though against yourselves or your parents or your relatives. Whether a man be rich or poor, God is his greater well-wisher than you. So follow not the behests of lust lest you swerve from justice; and if you prevaricate or avoid (giving evidence), God is cognisant of all that you do" (Q.IV:135); (2) fear of the enemy, "Oh you who believe, stand up as witnesses for God in all fairness, and do not let the hatred of a people deviate you from justice. Be just: This is closest to piety..." (Q.V:8)

In an Islamic system of justice, the responsibility of administering justice lies with (1) the government, (2) believers, and (3) all of mankind. The almighty Allah has addressed each of these classes specifically so that justice can be established to the fullest extent in the world. Thus, "Oh you who believe, be custodians of justice (and) witnesses for God..." (Q.IV:135). "Oh you who believe, stand up as witnesses for God..." (Q.V:8) "God enjoins that you render to the owners what is held in trust with you, and that when you judge among the people, do so equitably. Noble are the counsels of God, and God hears all and sees everything" (Q.IV:58). "Verily God has enjoined justice, the doing of good, and the giving of gifts to your relatives; and forbidden indecency, impropriety and oppression. He warns you that you may remember" (Q.XVI:90). It is, therefore, submitted that the state authorities must establish justice in their administration. The judiciary must establish justice in deciding cases and likewise, each and every member of the Islamic society is required to establish justice in his day-to-day affairs, or in dealing with others.

In Islam it is not only an obligation for all to do justice, but rather seeking to do justice is considered to be a part of worship. According to the Prophet, "An hour spent in the administration of justice is more valuable than sixty years spent in prayers." These characteristics of the extended obligation of rendering justice from the government to the individual, and the religious as well as secular bases of the conception of justice mark Islam's conception of justice distinctly.

Islamic justice is not a blind justice. While applying the law proper, it does not forget the hardships that may arise out of it. Thus, it is observed, "Verily God has enjoined justice, the doing of good, and the giving of gifts to your relatives..." (Q.XVI:90). Justice in its comprehensive sense, as 'Abd-Allah Yusuf 'Ali puts it in the notes of his translation of the *Qur'an* for this verse, "may include all the virtues of cold Philosophy" but Islam asks for "something warmer and more human." This "something warmer" is called *ihsan*, or goodness proper. *'Adl simpliciter* according to the Islamic concept is the doing of good for good, but *ihsan* is the doing of good even where *'adl* does not strictly demand it, and there is no question of receiving any reciprocal benefit. Justice, according to the command of Allah has, therefore, also to be tempered with mercy and it is on this principle that an otherwise legal claim may be withheld or a legal obligation not imposed upon considerations of hardship or the best interests of the community as a whole.[17]

Islam does not only provide a worldly mechanism for the establishment of justice but at the same time maintains a high moral, ethical and religious sentiment within the society which encourages everyone in administering justice. It speaks of the commission of justice in this world as well as final justice in the world hereafter. The one who avoids the Islamic worldly justice is bound to face the final justice of the life hereafter. Thus, 'Abd-Allah bin 'Umar bin al-'As narrates that once *Caliph* Abu Bakr rose to deliver his address and said, "Deposit *Sadaqa* for your camels tomorrow. I shall distribute it, and nobody should come to me without permission." Having heard this, a woman told her husband, "Have this nose-string; may Allah give us a camel." That person arrived at the spot and found Abu Bakr and 'Umar reaching the camels. He also followed them. The *Caliph* Abu Bakr turned towards him and asked, "Who made you enter the area?" And taking the nose-string, he struck him with it. When Abu Bakr became free from distributing the camels, he called the man near and giving back his nose-string said to him, "Take your revenge on me." 'Umar intervened and said, "By Allah he would not take his revenge and make it a practice." Abu Bakr said, "Who will save me from Allah on the Day of Judgement?" He then asked his slave to give the person his (Abu Bakr's) she-camel meant for riding, its saddle, a stripped blanket and five dinars and thus brought agreement.[18]

Justice in Islam is a bond which holds society together and transforms it into one brotherhood, every member of which is considered as a keeper unto every other and accountable for the welfare of all.

'Umar, the second *Caliph* of Islam, wrote a letter to Abu Musa al-Ash'ari, judge of Basra, highlighting the different aspects of Islamic justice as follows:

> Today, the office of the judge is a definite religious duty and a generally followed practice. Understand the depositions that are made before you, for it is useless to consider a Plea that is not valid.
>
> Consider all the people equal before you in your court and in your attention, so that the noble will not expect you to be partial, and the humble will not despair of justice from you.
>
> The claimant must produce evidence; from the defendant, an oath may be exacted. Compromise is permissible among the Muslims, but

---

17. Hamood al-Rahman, *The Concept of Justice in Islam*, in *Shari'a and Legal Profession* (S.M.Haider ed., 1985), pp. 169-70 .
18. Maulana Muhammad Yusuf Kandhlawi, *Hayat al-Sahabah, (The Lives of the Companions [of the Prophet])*(1985), Vol. 2, pp. 106-07.

not any agreement through which something forbidden is permitted, or something permitted is forbidden.

If you gave a judgment yesterday, and today, upon reconsideration, you come to the correct opinion, you should not hesitate by your first judgment from retracting; for justice is primeval, and it is better to retract than to persist in worthlessness.

Use your brain about matters that perplex you and to which neither the *Qur'an* nor the *Sunna* seems to apply. Study similar cases and evaluate the situation through analogy.

If a person brings a claim which he may or may not be able to prove, set a time limit for him. If he brings proof within the time limit, you should allow his claim; otherwise, you are permitted to give judgment against him. This is the better way to forestall or clear up any possible doubt.

All believers are acceptable as witnesses against each other, except such as have received a punishment provided for by the religious law, such as are proved to have given false witness, and such as are suspected of partiality on the ground of client status or relationship, for God, praised be He, forgives because of oath and postpones punishment in face of evidence.

Avoid fatigue and weariness and annoyance at the litigants. For establishing justice in the courts of justice, God will grant you a rich reward and give you a good reputation, Farewell.[19]

Thus, the letter emphasizes certain doctrines of Islamic justice such as due attention to the deposition, equal protection of law irrespective of status, burden of proof lies with the claimant, review of a judgement if found to be incorrect, application of analogical reasoning (*qiyas*) in cases not covered by the *Qur'an* and the *Sunna*, prescription, verification of the veracity of witness, *inter alia*.

The minorities also enjoy equal protection of law under Islamic justice. Thus, once the *Caliph* 'Ali lost a coat-of-mail belonging to him on his way to Siffin. After the termination of the war he returned to *al-Kufa*, and there he saw his armour in the hands of a Jew, and told him : "This armour is mine; I neither sold it nor gave it away." The Jew replied, "It is my armour and in my possession." Later, both the *Caliph* and the Jew went to the court of Shurayh. Shurayh said: "Proceed, O prince of the Faithful." He said: "Yes, this armour which is in the hands of this Jew is my armour-I neither sold it nor gave it away." Shurayh exclaimed, "What dost thou say, O Jew?" He replied: "It is my armour and in my possession." Then Shurayh said: "Hast thou any proof, O Prince of the Faithful?" He said: "Yes, *Kambar* and al-Hasan ('Ali's son) are witnesses to

---

19. Anwar Ahmad Qadri, *Justice in Historical Islam* (1980), p. 20.

the fact that the armour is mine." Shurayh replied, "The evidence of a son is not admissible in favour of the father." The result was that the judgement was given in favour of the Jew. At this, the Jew exclaimed, "I testify that there is no god but God, Muhammad is His Apostle, and that this armour is thy armour."[20]

Some more aspects of the conception of Islamic justice will be examined in the course of later discussion.

COMPARATIVE STUDY

The conception of justice, in Western jurisprudence, appears to revolve around the question whether law should reflect morality or not. The dichotomy is between what the law "is" and what the law "ought to be", theoretically between positive law and natural law. Thus, from the very beginning Plato, in his theory of justice, emphasizes morality while Aristotle emphasizes the law. Most of the subsequent Western philosophers have either joined Plato or Aristotle in formulating their concept of justice. The renowned English jurist John Austin and Hans Kelsen of the Vienna school also separate justice from law. According to Austin, "the science of jurisprudence is concerned with positive laws, or with laws strictly so called, as considered without regard to their goodness or badness."[21] Hans Kelsen's pure theory of law is also an attempt to separate morality from law. According to Kelsen, "The task of legal theory is to clarify the relations between the fundamental and all lower norms, but not to say whether this fundamental norm itself is good or bad. That is the task of political science, or of ethics or of religion."[22]

Western Naturalists, on the other hand, emphasize on the joining of law with morality. Thus, to Stammler, the idea of law is the realization of justice.[23] St. Augustine and St. Thomas Aquinas considered justice to be the overriding objective of the law and consequently came to the conclusion that an unjust law lacked the attribute of a law.[24] Salmond defines law in terms of justice, so that "the law may be defined as the body of principles recognized and applied by the state in the administration of justice. In other words, the law consists of the rules recognized and acted on by courts."[25] Dias remarks:

> [The Positivists] maintain, every proposition-which passes through one or other of the accepted media (i.e. precedent, legislation and

---

20. *Id.* at 27-28.
21. John Austin, *Lectures on Jurisprudence: or, The Philosophy of Positive Law* (4th ed., Campbell, 1876), pp.182-83.
22. Friedmann, *supra* note 1, at 277.
23. Bodenheimer, *supra* note 13, at 128.
24. *Id.* at 212.
25. John William Salmond, *Jurisprudence* (7th ed.), p. 39.

immemorial customs) is law irrespective of all considerations which go towards saying that it should be, or should not be law...Natural lawyers would assert that a proposition is law not merely because it satisfies some formal requirement, but by virtue of an additional minimum moral content. According to them an immoral rule would not be law, however much it may satisfy formal requirements.[26]

Therefore, Western theories of justice conceptualize the issues of law and morality as contradictions to one another and fail to present a uniform idea of justice.

Islamic theories of justice on the other hand, present the issues of law and morality in a uniform and harmonious manner. Given revelation, as the common source of law and morality, there is no contradiction as such in the Islamic theories of justice. Law is not considered in isolation of the issues of morality. Rather, the issues of law and morality overlap one another. Theoretically, the Islamic justice system contains both the positivist and naturalist aspects of Western justice system.

The question of stability and change has also been an issue of controversy in the Western theories of justice. The analytical positivists emphasize "what the law is," that is, on the static aspect of law, whereas the naturalists and pragmatic positivists emphasize "what the law ought to be", that is, on the changing aspect of law. Friedmann remarks:

> From a different angle, Savingny's historical school opposes legal changes. For this school the task of a jurist and the legislator is to verify and formulate existing legal customs; the function of law is essentially to stabilize, not to be an agent of progress; analytical positivism, by its emphasis on logic and obedience to written law, tends to regard stability and certainty as the paramount objects of legal interpretation. On the other hand, all utilitarian and sociological theories tend to emphasize the changing aspects of law because they see it against its social background and the needs of life. The ways to attain pleasure and avoid pain change with social circumstances, so the law must change with them.[27]

Although this inconsistency exists in Western theories of justice, justice demands that a legal system should possess both the qualities of stability and change. Roscoe Pound observes, "law must be stable and yet it cannot stand still."[28] Edgar Bodenheimer similarly observes, "both the backward pull and the forward push are essential to the proper working of any legal system."[29]

---

26. Reginald Walter Michael Dias, *Jurisprudence* (5th ed. 1985), p. 332.
27. Friedmann, *supra* note 1, at 86-87.
28. Roscoe Pound, *Interpretations of Legal History* (Cambridge, Mass., 1923), p. 1.
29. Bodenheimer, *supra* note 13, at 220.

Islamic legal theory contains principles which provide for both stability and change. In Islam, there are some immutable basic legal principles as well as an ethical code of good and bad which keep the legal structure stable within the bound although having at the same time enough space for accommodating new changes by the application of the doctrine of *qiyas*, principles of equity, and the rule of necessity and need in proper cases.

Western jurisprudence, in search for absolute justice, relied in turn on natural law theories and positive law theories but neither could successfully provide the foundation for absolute justice. Positive law, being divorced from ideals of justice, could not satisfy the demand of just law. If law is not based on morality, it may become tyrannical and oppressive to the people and might lead to a revolt against the authority and disturb the social balance. A demand for something more than mere application of statute or precedent was felt necessary and therefore, Western legal theory relied on natural law; but natural law, being based on reason, received different meanings in the hands of different scholars. Reason varies from man to man. Hume criticized "reason" as a "slave of passions",[30] while Kant, in his *Critique of Pure Reason*, has also shown the limitations of reason.

Reason is subject to error and therefore cannot be a reliable source of knowledge. It is reason, which has resulted in conflicting views about justice. Absolute justice cannot be known rationally. It is God alone who knows what is absolutely good and just. Revelation is, therefore, the perfect source of knowledge of good and evil. Almighty Allah possesses the absolute and perfect knowledge. "You may dislike a thing: yet, it may be good for you; or you may love a thing but it may be bad for you. Only God has knowledge, and you do not know" (Q.II:216). "And they [the angels] said, Glory to you (Oh Lord), knowledge we have none, except what You have given us, for You are all-knowing and all-wise" (Q.II:32). We have, therefore, to depend upon revelation which is the only source of genuine knowledge. Revelation is the word of God, transmitted to the Prophet Muhammad whose integrity and veracity are beyond doubt (Q.LXXI:19-21). The *Shari'a* is based upon revelation which is the only reliable source of the knowledge of things, their goodness and badness. Friedmann therefore rightly observes, "The history of Natural law is a tale of the search of mankind for absolute justice and of its failure."[31] He further observes:

> The different schools of Neo-Kantian philosophers have realized the relativity of justice and the dualism between eternal justice and positive law. They have, therefore, divorced the idea of justice from positive law. Some have refused to study the varying contents of the

---

30. Friedmann, *supra* note 1, at 130.
31. *Id.* at 95.

idea of justice as irrelevant to legal science (Vienna school). Alternatively, they have formulated the main conflicting ideals of justice (Radbruch) or attempted in vain to fill the formal ideal of justice with a substantial content (Stammler). What emerges from all these varying attempts is the failure to establish absolute standards of justice except on a religious basis.[32]

Unlike the extreme Western theories of justice providing either unrestricted power to the state and limited freedom to the individuals (Plato, totalitarianism), or unrestricted freedom to the individuals and limited power to the state (Stoics, Hobbes),[33] the Islamic theory of justice provides a balance between the two. Muhammad Muslih al-Din observes that Islam:

> ... seeks not to crush the liberty of the individual but to control it in favour of society which includes the individual himself, and thus protects his legitimate interests too. Law plays its part in reconciling the interests of the individual with those of society and vice versa. The individual is allowed to develop his personality with the only proviso that he should not come into conflict with the interests of society. This puts an end to friction and satisfies the claims of justice.[34]

Both the Western and Islamic conceptions of justice have many common elements, including:

Dignity of the human person

Islamic justice is based on the dignity of the human person. "It is He who made you trustees on the earth..."(Q.VI:165). Man is a trustee of the Almighty on earth (Q.II:30). In Islam, the whole of creation is for man's benefit, but man is created to obey his Lord. After the creation of Adam, the first man, all the angels were ordered to bow down before him (Adam) which implies that man's superiority among the creation is willed by the Almighty Allah, but it has been made clear in the *Qur'an* time and again that this superiority is conditional on his attaining Islamic qualities of justice irrespective of factors such as race, colour, language, status, *inter alia*. The Western conception of justice also recognizes the dignity of the human person.

Fundamental human rights

The Islamic justice system ensures fundamental human rights, such as the

---

32. *Id.* at 346.
33. *Id.* at 88-90.
34. Muhammad Muslih al-Din, *Philosophy of Islamic law and the Orientalists: a Comparative Study of Islamic Legal System* (Lahore, Islamic Publications 1977), p. 106.

right to life, right to property, freedom of movement, freedom of speech, among others. Thus, "And do not take a life, which God has forbidden, except in a just cause" (Q.XVII:33). In Islam the "right to life" is so sacred that if anyone has saved a life, it would be as if he had saved the life of the whole people of the world. Similarly, Islam teaches that if a man has taken a life, without just cause and due process of law, it would be as if he had killed the whole of humanity. (Q.V:32). Islam also guarantees freedom of expression, "Those who believe...enjoin what is proper and prohibit what is wrong"(Q.IX:71). The right to privacy is also recognized, "Oh you who believe, do not enter other houses except yours without first seeking permission..." (Q.XXIV:27).

The American Declaration of Independence (1776) states that all men are created equal, and among their inalienable rights are life, liberty and the pursuit of happiness.[35] The American Bill of Rights consists of ten amendments added in 1791 to the Federal Constitution of 1787. These rights include free exercise of religion, freedom of speech and the press;[36] security of persons, houses, papers and effects from unreasonable searches and seizures;[37] the prohibition against deprivation of life, liberty or property without due process of law;[38] and freedom from excessive bail or fines and from cruel or unusual punishments.[39] Later amendments abolished slavery,[40] and preserved the right to vote from discrimination on grounds of race, colour or sex.[41] The constitutions of individual American states also contain Bills of Rights.[42] A Declaration of the Rights of man was prefaced to the French Constitution of 1791,[43] and was confirmed by the preambles to the constitutions of 1946 and 1958. Basic liberties were also treated in the European Convention on Human Rights (1950).[44]

Principles of Natural Justice

Islamic justice follows all the principles of natural justice, which were incorporated into the Islamic justice system through the direct revelation of Almighty Allah. These include, for example, requirements that judges make

---

35. THE DECLARATION OF INDEPENDENCE (U.S. 1776), para. 2.
36. U.S. CONST. amend. I.
37. U.S. CONST. amend. IV.
38. U.S. CONST. amend. V.
39. U.S. CONST. amend. VIII.
40. U.S. CONST. amend. XIII.
41. U.S. CONST. amend. XV.
42. *See, eg.,* TEX. CONST. Art. I.
43. DECLARATION OF THE RIGHTS OF MAN AND OF THE CITIZEN, (approved by the National Assembly of France, Aug. 26, 1789).
44. O. Hood Phillips and Paul Jackson, *O. Hood Phillips' Constitutional and Administrative Law*(London, Sweet & Maxwell, 6th ed. 1984), pp. 16-17.

decisions without favor and fear (Q.IV:135, Q.V:8); judge with justice (Q.IV:58); the presumption of innocence (Q.XXIV:12-13); the affirmative defenses of compelled action (Q.XVI:106) and self-defense (Q.XLII:41); personal responsibility for culpable actions (Q.XLII:15, Q.XXXIX:7); and the right of the defendant to be heard (Q.LXXXII:11, Q.XXXIX:69, Q.XXIV:24).

Principles of natural justice form part of procedural justice. If these principles are not observed strictly, then the decision of the court, substantive justice, may result in injustice. Therefore, in addition to substantive justice, the Islamic system emphasizes the observance of the principles of natural justice. In Western countries, the courts follow these principles also as an aspect of procedural justice. For the non-observance of any of these principles, an appellate court may set aside the decision of a lower court or tribunal.

Constitutional supremacy (Qur'anic legislation) and the principles of judicial review

Islamic divine law, as the supreme law, requires that any dispute between the individual and the State will be settled in the light of divine law. It is the function of the highest court to decide whether an act of the government agrees to the divine law or not. This is the same principle by which the validity of any statute is tested. This principle used to be followed even in the formative period of Islam. Zayd bin Aslam narrates:

> The house of 'Abbas bin Abd al-Mutallib was situated beside the *Masjid al-Madina*.[45] 'Umar, during his administration, asked him to sell his house to him for he wanted to bring about some extension in the boundary of the *Masjid*. 'Abbas refused to do so. 'Umar then asked him to give the house as a gift to him. 'Abbas refused to accept this too. 'Umar then asked him to bring about extension into the boundaries of the *Masjid* through that house. 'Abbas refused to accept it as well. Then 'Umar suggested that someone be put as an arbitrator between them. 'Abbas named Ubay bin Ka'b, and 'Umar accepted him. Both of them brought their dispute to Ubay bin Ka'b. He said to 'Umar "You can not turn him out from the house without his ('Abbas's) consent." 'Umar said, "Have you taken this decision from the Book of Allah? Or you have found it somewhere in the *sun'na* of the Holy Prophet? Ubay bin Ka'b said, "I have given this judgement rather from the *Sunna* of the Holy Prophet." 'Umar said, "What is that *Sunna?"* He said, "I have heard the Prophet saying. 'While Sulaiman bin Dawud was constructing "Bayt al-Maqdis", he would see the wall

---

45. *Tr.* "Mosque in Medina".

demolished every time he got it raised. Then Allah revealed to Sulaiman that a building must not be constructed on any body else's land without his consent.'" At this, 'Umar gave up this dispute. 'Abbas then extended the boundary of the *Masjid* by giving his own house.[46]

This principle was first recognized in the U.S. Supreme Court, under the influence of Chief Justice Marshall in the case of *Marbury v. Madison*[47] and *Fletcher v. Peck*.[48] In the United States each state as well as the federal government has a well-delineated constitutional structure. The state courts have jurisdiction to declare state legislation repugnant to the state constitution; and the federal courts have jurisdiction to declare provisions of state constitutions, state legislation and federal legislation repugnant to the federal constitution.[49] Many European States utilize a special constitutional court, as provided for in the constitutions of the Republic of Cyprus, West Germany and Italy.[50] In Britain however, legislative Supremacy is practiced. There is no written constitution or formal higher law binding on Parliament and therefore, the courts have no power to "review" acts of Parliament and declare them unconstitutional.[51]

Rule of law

In the Islamic system of justice everybody is subjected to the rule of law. No one is above the law and immune from the law, including the head of a state or government. It does not recognize the Western concepts such as the "King can do no wrong" or "sovereign immunity." The Prophet himself appeared in several suits filed against him.[52] He established the important constitutional principles that the head of any Islamic state could be sued both as a private individual and also in respect of his public acts. During the last Sermon of Hujjat al-Widaa, he in fact testified to his love for justice and equality, by publicly declaring to the congregation that any one having any claim against him may make it so that he may discharge the same. This principle of equal applicability of the law was also in force during the *Rashidun Caliphs*. (the Rightly-Guided *Caliphs*, i.e., the first four *Caliphs*).The first *Caliph*, on the assumption of his office, declared in his first sermon, "co-operate with me if I am right, set me right if I go astray. The weaker among you will be strong with me till his right has been vindicated, and the strong among you will be weak

---

46. Kandhlawi, *supra* note 18, at 108-09.
47. Marbury v. Madison, 5 U.S. (1 Cranch.) 137 (1803)(Marshall, C.J.).
48. Fletcher v. Peck, 10 U.S. (6 Cranch.) 87 (1810).
49. U.S. CONST. art. VI, cl. 2. *See also*, Cooper v. Aaron, 358 U.S. 1 (1958).
50. Phillips, *supra* note 46, at 8-9.
51. *Id.* at 26-27.
52. K. Jamil Ahmed, *Heritage of Islam* 259

with me till I have taken what is due from him. Obey me as long as I obey God and His Prophet. If I disobey Him and His Prophet, obey me not."[53]

Once, a woman belonging to a noble family of Madina was arrested in connection with a theft. The case was brought before the Prophet, and it was requested that she might be spared. The Prophet replied, "The nations that lived before you were destroyed by God because they punished the common men for their offences but let their dignitaries go unpunished for their crimes. I swear by Him (God) Who holds my life in His hand that even if Fatima, the daughter of Muhammad, had committed this crime, then I would have amputated her hand." The Prophet has been reported to have said: "Give equitable punishment to the remote and the near and have no fear of reproach of people in enforcement of his limits set up by God."[54]

Dicey in the *Law of the Constitution*, explains the term "rule of law" as comprising three concepts: (a) the absence of arbitrary power – no man is above the law; (b) equality before the law – every man, whatever his rank or condition, is subject to the ordinary law; and (c) the general principles of the British constitution, in particular the conception of individual liberties.[55] These principles are common to Western societies.

Separation of Powers

The Islamic conception of justice recognizes the principle of separation of powers into three branches of government with proper checks and balance. In Islam, the judiciary is given complete freedom from executive interference. In the United States this principle is also followed so that any particular branch of the government may not become tyrannical.[56] Both systems are in harmony regarding the need to avoid the concentration of excessive power in any body or individual.[57]

Peace and security.

One of the important objects of Islamic justice system is to maintain peace and security. Thus "God does not love those who are corrupt" (Q.V:64), "[D]o not be aggressive: God does not like aggressors" (Q.II:190). Western societies also seek to maintain peace and security through the administration of justice.

---

53. Justice Gul Muhammad Khan, *The Concept of Justice in Islam,* in *Shari'a and Legal Profession* (S.M. Haider ed. 1985), pp. 214-215.
54. Shaikh Shaukat Hussain, *Human Rights in Islam* (1990), p. 63.
55. Phillips, *supra* note 46, at 36.
56. *See, e.g.*, Youngstown Sheet & Tube Co. V. Sawyer, 343 U.S. 579 (1952) (discussing the limits of Presidential power).
57. Phillips, *supra* note 46, at 14.

CONCLUSION

The conception of justice may be regarded as a mirror of a society which reflects the whole face of that society – its social, legal, political, and moral aspects, *inter alia*. Since the fundamental assumptions on which a society is rooted vary from society to society, the conception of justice at the outset appears to be different in type and nature.

The conception of justice is perhaps as old as human civilization. Whatever may be the origin of the conception of justice, reason or revelation, throughout the ages of human civilization there has always been a striving to achieve justice according to the level of intellectual maturity of each society. It is a historical reality that in every stage of human development the realization of justice has been an impetus for further societal change and development. Although as a natural corollary of intellectual diversity, different approaches to the conception of justice have arisen, there are certain elements which remain common to all; a system of justice which has the qualities of positivism and idealism, stability and change, individualism and collectivism, among other values may fulfill the demand of justice properly. Western systems of justice reflect many of these qualities in common with the Islamic system of justice.

Western theories of justice present different approaches to the conception of justice some of which are contradictory to one another although representing the same school of legal thought. Individual scholars and jurists have formulated their own theories of justice – some of which have tremendously influenced the administration of justice of their times, while appearing provocative to succeeding generations, but others have come out as mere reactions to the prevailing justice system of their times. The natural law theory of justice in the 20th century appears to have lost its original character of idealism and universality and has been changed with the change of social and political conditions. Attempts to establish universal principles of justice by the rationalist theorists of natural law on the basis of reason have been attacked by Hume. He demonstrates that reason is the slave of the passions which alone inspire human action. Neo-Kantian philosophers, considering the relativity of justice and dualism between eternal justice and positive law, have separated the idea of justice from positive law. Therefore, all attempts to establish absolute standards of justice appear to have failed except on a religious basis.

Reason being fallible, the Islamic conception of justice takes revelation as its base. The Almighty Allah is perfect in knowledge and wisdom (Q.II:32). Revelation is, therefore, considered to be the most reliable source of knowledge about good and evil, the just and unjust. In Islam there appears to be no dichotomy among law, morality, rights. Rather the theory of justice explains everything in the light of one divine scheme with no confusion left in it. Although Western and Islamic conceptions of justice have some fundamental differences, there are certain elements which they share in common, such as the dignity of human person, fundamental human rights, principles of natural justice, the rule of law, peace and security, *inter alia,* and these principles reflect the rules of common legal behaviour between the West and Islam.

Justice in the Islamic Shari'a

Muhammad Fathi Al-Dirini[1]

The concept of justice in legislation – any legislation – is based on the general legal and social theories from which it derives its specific provisions, including general principles and structured societal objectives as well as concerns for "human rights" of all types, along with their limits and applicability.

The "Supreme Legitimacy Principle" of the legislation focuses on the "Pivotal Value" on which the legislation in its entirety is dependent, representing a mandatory moral imperative that may not be disobeyed, or contractually derogated from, and which, as an underlying societal value, is supreme to the dependent legislation.

However, the "pivotal value" defines a "concept of right" in each legislative act, as an individual liberty whereby the subject may act as he deems fit according to his volition, regardless of its direction, for the realization of his self-interest without taking into consideration the correlative interests of other individuals, those of the society, or of the State as a sovereign entity.

Accordingly, this theory of legislation implies that "justice" should be an "individualized concept" to reflect the absolute discretion of the individual in its application, according to the individual subject's free will.

Moreover, this view would hold that "the right" is a purely social concept, transforming an absolute into a mere social function, and the subject possesses this right for societal purposes.

Therefore, "the right" represents nothing more than a mere social position to be assigned to its possessor for the performance of his altruistic pursuits without regard for self-interest. As such, an interest which is detrimental to this right is *altruistic*, rather than *egoistic*. This social model is completely

---

[1]. Professor of Jurisprudence and Islamic Law, University of Jordan; Former Dean of the Faculty of Islamic Law, Damascus University.

contrary to the former "pivotal values" conception, as it basically eliminates the idea of right from legislation.

Nevertheless, we may observe that the exercise of an absolute individualist orientation toward the concept of rights is extremism, for it sacrifices the broader societal interest thus making the concept of justice suffer from selectivity, factionalism, or diminution. Furthermore, to be entirely oriented toward the public interest without regard for the individual interest, is extremism as well, as absolute sacrifice of the individual interest sacrifices basic human rights, and legislation that abuses human rights fails the interest of justice.

It is possible that the concept of "the right" represents a conceptual duality – whereby legislation imposes on the subject a duty to observe the interest of others in the exercise of his own interest, whether the subject may be an individual citizen, a society, or the State. Such legislation will allow neither interest to take precedence over the other, considering this an express injustice, thus avoiding extremism and showing a tendency to balance the mechanisms of the State for the mutual benefit of the individual and society. A State exercising this equilibrium will maintain that the "concept of justice" is inherent in maintaining balanced interests. It is obvious, however, that in balancing interests, the State will inevitably give first priority to the public interest, while abrogating the interest of the individual to the least extent possible.

Such a balance of interests, with ultimate preeminence for societal concerns, is ordained by Islamic *Shari'a*. "Justice" in the *Shari'a* – according to the view of many legal scholars and commentators, does not represent an abstract and philosophical intellectual concept incompatible with the essence of the legislation; but the legislation, its rules, provisions and purposes, promote the moral and material needs of society while recognizing natural aspirations of values and ideals.

This concept of justice in the *Shari'a* is clearly revealed in the objectives of its practical provisions and general rules. Scholars refer to these as the "objectives" or "interests" served by such legislation, as each practical provision or general rule has, as its object, the promotion of a tangible societal interest. Recognition of the interests to be furthered by a given piece of legislation should always be a primary interpretive guideline. A wise legislator takes these interests into account in framing "legislative commandments" as a means to achieving a desired goal, while carefully avoiding ambiguity which might give rise to the exercise of pure philosophical speculation in statutory interpretation.

There are therefore many legislative commandments – in the *Qur'an* and the *Sunna* which are "correlated" or associated with the "warrants" and reasons which underlie their legislation, or which refer to the societal interests which are the object of such commandments. These warrants and reasons attempt to manifest the logic or reasonableness of the legislation in conjunction with the legislation's feasibility and necessity, such that its implementation and compliance will be volitional acts driven by society's firm belief in the righteousness of the legislation.

On the basis of this argument, we conclude that if the commandments of the *Qur'an* and the *Sunna,* and the total rules included therein, were the core of justice; *a priori,* the "purposes" intended from legislation and the "objectives" such commandments and rules are seeking to achieve fall in the sphere of "justice" as a first principle, given the primacy of the ends to the means as the basis of reason and law.

Consequently, the *Qur'an,* confirmed by the *Sunna,* is concerned with the implementation of the law or application of the rules on a given set of facts. This is precisely "on point" as an example for the legislator seeking to achieve a particular objective, as it represents the exercise of "justice" in its most magnificent form. Under no circumstances will a wise legislator allow implementation of a legal judgement in a manner which may be inconsistent with the interest to be furthered.

The most eminent scholars are in accord with this position, and that such actions should be considered void *ab initio.* In this regard, al-Shattibi in his valuable book, *Agreements in Shari'a Principles (Muwafakat),* noted that "He who seeks in the *Shari'a* assignments [of] things other than what they have been enacted for, contradicts…[the] *Shari'a,* and accordingly this contradictory action is void and so [is] its result."[2] He further states that "The legislator meant that the assignee's aim from the action should be in agreement with Allah's purpose from legislation."

This demonstrates that the legal judgement, which itself is the origin of the right, is concerned with the end legally planned for it, and that the right is not an end in it self, as is characteristic of extreme individualism. However, Al-Shattibi held that "reasoning" for the sake of inference of the warrant from the provision dictating the legal judgement thereof, is a persistent element inherent throughout the *Shari'a.* "What has been confirmed is that we have inferred from the *Shari'a,* that it has been established for the interests of mankind, this induction is not indisputable[3] and if induction indicated as such, and was useful to science in this matter, then we definitely conclude that the subject matter is persistent in the *Shari'a*…as a whole."[4]

However, the *Qur'an* may be interpreted according to the underlying philosophy implied in the principle of enacting legislation concerning the judgment, but not just as a justification of the outcome. For example, the *Qur'an* speaks of retribution in the case of wounds (Q.V:45). Retribution is not the end to be accomplished, but rather the means to the end. The end to be served is the sanctity of one's "right to life." This legislative wisdom, the right to life, is at

---

2. Al-Imam Al-Shattibi, *Agreements in Shari'a Principles (Muwafakat)*, Vol. 2, p. 245.
3. *Id.,* at 245 *passim.*
4. *Id.* at 7.

the core of Islamic justice, and other legal penalties further this end, such as the death penalty for murder. Such penalties represent dual objectives of justice and deterrance.

A wise judge always considers what is the legitimate interest to be served in adjudicating on the basis of individual facts, and where there is no clear rule, the interest should be paramount in reasoning by analogy. Nevertheless, ambiguity must not be asserted in an attempt to contradict totally confirmed rules or detailed and conclusive legislative pronouncements.

Adjudicating on the basis of significant recognizable "interests" does not violate the spirit of *Shari'a*, but rather this process elaborates on the underlying concepts of justice. This is consistent with realism in *Shari'a* realism, achieving the essential interests of the community of believers. In this context Ibn Qayyem al-Jawziya says: "[w]herever the interest is realized, there will be the commandment (judgement) and Religion of Allah."[5] Undoubtedly, Allah's commandments and religion represent "Justice" as a matter of logical necessity.

This ability to identify the essential interests and reason by analogy in matters not clearly provided for textually is a matter which has been entrusted to diligent *Shari'a* scholars, consequently in Islam judicial scholarship is closely associated with justice, because it is the practical means by which justice is recognized in theory and observed in reality and practice. Thus, human reason enables the *Shari'a* to remain vibrant and relevant in contemporary society, and this is what Al-Imam al-Ghazali referred to by saying: "The noblest of sciences is the one which combines both opinion and the commandment (*Shari'a*), as it is neither a conduct of pure reason, not acceptable to the *Shari'a* nor a conduct of pure imitation - with no diligence in opinion - receiving no support or consideration from reason."[6]

Diligence in *Shari'a* scholarship becomes a collective duty on the Islamic State. The necessity of establishing justice as a duty in itself has been treated in detail in the *Qur'an* and the confirmed *Sunna*. We find imperative statements in Islam which call for the concept of justice to become the essence of the human soul, to be the source of reason and action in society. "O you who believe, stand up as witnesses for God in all fairness, and do not let the hatred of a people deviate you from justice. Be just: This is closest to piety: and beware of God. Surely God is aware of all you do" (Q.V:8).

Clearly, Allah has intended justice to be a natural part of the souls of the believers, which naturally guides their actions and spontaneously, allowing the justice of Allah to spring forth without difficulty in judgment. He did not say "*You* must establish justice", but rather that believers are to "stand up as witnesses for *God*," and therefore, let justice emanate as a matter of divine

---

5. *Informing the Signatories*.
6. Al Mustasfi, *Imam Ghazali*, Vol. I, p. 4.

will. Moreover, as justice is a matter of divine will, it is to be applied impartially, as Allah the Almighty states: "And do not let your hatred of a people...lead you to aggression. [H]elp one another in goodness and piety..." (Q.V:3). Therefore, piety (duty)[7] is one of the strongest forms of pure and sincere worship in Islam, and being just is a means of worshiping Allah. In Islam there should be no separation of worship and justice – the establishment of a just society is for the sake of Allah, the Almighty.

Because the integrity of human society is based on justice, Allah created the interests to be served in the application of justice. Imam Shattibi states that "the interest as an interest intended for judgement is the legislator's concern, for if the legislator enacted the judgement for the sake of the interest, then he is the creator of the interest thereto, otherwise, and on the basis of reason, it could not be so."[8] The legislator should not substitute his own interest for the interest inspired by Allah.

Some may argue that given the variety of possible interests to be recognized, how is the legislator to identify legitimate interests? Allah is at the core of legitimate interests and it is He who formed their general concepts and established the rules and conditions through which diligent scholarship will enable them to be identified and applied for all times. Although the human mind is affected to a large extent by ethnic motives and desires, which hinder the application of straightforward logic, justice and supreme human interests should not be allowed to play a secondary role in enacting legislation.

The *Qur'anic* verses and *Sunna* reveal that the *raison d'être* of the revelation of the *Shari'a* releases people from the effects of their whims,[9] as Al-Imam al-Shattibi says:

> The *Qur'an* and the confirmed *Sunna* judgements came associated with the warrants, i.e. suspicions of interests, as the judgement and the interest sought from it are inseparable, in theory, application or practice. Deviation from the purpose of judgement during its application is considered religiously a taboo, [the judgment is] prohibited and the action is invalid. This means that these wasted "interests" represent the forms of "justice" in legislation, and such judgements were only enacted for the achievement of such interests being their objectives. Hence, judgement may not be separated from its purpose, as no feasibility is to be expected from a means if not leading to the only purpose for which the judgment was enacted.

For example, the *Qur'an* provides a set of priorities for inheritance rights, which provides for the payment of legacies without prejudice to the rights of

---

7. Sheikh Muhammad Abdou, *Al Manar Interpretation,* Vol. 5, p. 45.
8. Shattibi, *supra* note 1, at Vol. 2, p. 315.
9. *Id.*

others (Q.IV:11-12). The concern not to do injury in the fulfillment of a legal right demonstrates that the purpose of the law must always be taken into account in fulfilling its intent. Research in the provisions of the *Qur'an* and scholarly commentary reveals a wide recognition that the ends of justice are attained through attention to the means selected to accomplish the objective.

Al-Imam al-Shatibi developed a general rule that "the illegal purpose destroys the legal purpose"[10] which invalidates an otherwise legitimate action. It is clear that "justice" in Islam is concerned with both the judgement and the purpose of legislation. This should be taken into consideration, whether in the process of inference, or in practical application. The ends of fact-based judgement, based on ambiguous conditions, will have an effect on justice in legislation, as actions are evaluated by their results – negatively as well as positively. This is what Al-Imam al-Shatibi refers to by saying that a consideration of the ends or results of actions[11] is a legitimate means to avoid injurious consequences, or corrupt results. The *Shari'a* is not to be applied for a purpose which is totally forbidden both on the basis of reason and the *Shari'a*.

Therefore, we may conclude the following:

> *First*: The right or public freedom may not be used for a purpose other than the one originally prescribed for it, because this "contradicts" justice in legislation, as it separates the right from its purpose.
>
> *Second*: A "balance" should be established between the theoretical interest and the possibility of an unjust practical result, with a preference given for the outcome which is more socially beneficial, as this outcome will be closest to the intent of the legislator.
>
> *Third*: This necessitates that greater weight should be given to the public interest in case of contradictions with the individual interest, together with just compensation for the individual to ward off injury. While the realization of individual interest is a duty, the regard for the public interest is a duty as well in the *Shari'a* because it represents justice in its noblest form.
>
> In the light of the above, scholars classified rights into the following two basic categories:(1) The right of the individual human being; and (2) The right of the society - the public interest. The scholars termed the latter as "the right of Allah" in reference to how grave, important, and comprehensive this right was.[12]
>
> *Fourth*: The legal judgement — which is the origin of rights and freedoms — is attributed and interpreted in the light of the interest prescribed by the legislator, as a purpose thereof, and it is to be asso-

---

10. *Id.* at p. 386
11. *See* Dr. Fathi Al Dirini, *Abusive Use of the Right* p. 24 *passim*.
12. Shattibi, *supra* note 1, at Vol. 4, p. 196 *passim*.

ciated with it theoretically and practically, because it represents justice.

Fifth: If the application of a judgment will lead — in ambiguous conditions — to a most likely corruption exceeding the interest decided for it, then it must be legally forbidden even if the action itself was originally legal. In this regard, Al-Imam al-Shatibi says that the actor should be forbidden, regardless of purpose or psychological motives even if they were good. "Performing the cause[13] is equal to performing [the] effect (disposition of the right and the permission) whether it was intentional or not because he is considered as the direct doer in the light of the effect revealed in the course of customs."[14]

Hence, establishing the balance between interests served and possible unjust outcomes is a duty regardless of whether the initial action is legal or illegal, and regardless of psychological motives of good or evil because this balance between contradictory individual interests or and between public and private interests, is part of the principles of justice in Islam. Accordingly, we may observe that a diminution of public or private interests is a diminution of justice itself.

From this analysis of the concept of justice in Islam, we may conclude that "justice" in the *Shari'a* is expressed by observing "the right of others" in the exercise of individual rights or freedoms. Al-Imam al-Shattibi states that the rights of others are legally preserved, whether as an individual or society. Thus, the observation of the rights of others is a general principle required by "justice" in Islam, which permits the exercise of individual rights to the extent that they are not in conflict with objective societal values. The *Shari'a* ensures that its rules recognize this social meaning, inherent in the concept of rights and freedoms, which restrict their exercise, in order not to harm other individuals or society itself.

The nexus of justice and kindness in the *Qur'an* recognizes that both aspects of the good are interrelated, and that a strict application of legal justice may violate the *Qur'anic* duty of kindness. This is an interplay of the binding provisions of the *Shari'a* – justice and equity, and the moral judgments of the *Shari'a,* particularly when seen in the light of specific fact patterns. Each case dictates a certain pattern of justice, or a consideration of tolerance and kindness in accordance with the surrounding circumstances. These two elements — tolerance and kindness — represent pillars of justice which strengthen the social fabric of a just society.

This combination of justice and kindness in the *Shari'a* may be seen in the *Qur'an*, which states: "Pay homage to God…and be good to your parents and

---

13. *See* the books of principles under chapter: *The Sentenced.*
14. Shattibi, *supra* note 1, at Vol. 3, p. 358 *passim.*

relatives…"(Q.4:36). Al-Imam al-Izz bin 'Abd al-Salam considers this to be "[t]he most comprehensive verse in the *Qur'an*", incorporating both justice and kindness. As Al-Imam al-Ezz says: "Nothing remains of 'kindness' (*Ihsan*) delicacy and essence unless included entirely in kindness as well as justice."

These principles must guide all aspects of human life, for even an small breach of justice invites further abuses. This is why the *Shari'a* is concerned with the establishment of justice and kindness, in all ordinary and exceptional matters, great and small alike. This requirement applies equally to those in authority and ordinary citizens, however, such leniency is inapplicable to religious virtues.[15] For example, the *Qur'an* provides how creditors should deal with debtors in difficult economic circumstances and does not permit creditors to pursue their claims while the debtor is insolvent. Furthermore, the *Qur'an* urges the affluent creditor to write off his debts, partially or totally, as a matter of charity. "If a debtor is in want, give him time until his circumstances improve; but if you forego (the debt) as charity, that will be to your good, if you really understand" (Q.II:280). Al-Imam bin al-Izz bin 'Abd ul-Salam emphasizes that "kindness either brings benefit or prevents damage."[16]

Kindness, therefore, is a core concept of justice, which provides a moral or equitable basis for its application. The *Shari'a* applies the rules of justice in a manner to achieve their moral objective, as Islamic law is based on religious principles of justice and morality.[17] In *Shari'a*, the rules of law are inseparable from the moral rules, and therefore, a just law is also a moral obligation.

The well-known French scholar, Professor Joesrah, refers to this nexus of law and morality when he says, "[b]orders between law and morality exist only in the imagination of some scholars, and the evidence for this is in the definitions they gave for these two sciences in the context of explaining the difference between them." The failure to recognize the common basis of these concepts ignores that they have common origins – as the principles of law are but the principles of morals, and ethics is no more than the crucible in which law is formulated through legislation, tradition, and custom.[18]

This is but an objective criticism, based on the *Shari'a*, and it is confirmed by the well-known French professor, Ribier, who states in his book about the moral rule in civil liabilities that "[t]here is no difference between the law and morality, neither in terms of purpose nor in terms of scope, as all rules are governed by morals, providing them with legitimacy and obligation in the souls of individuals, and making them more acceptable and adequate for practical application."[19]

---

15. *Id.*
16. Al-Imam ben al-Izz ben 'Abdul-Salam, *The Rules of Judgments*; *see also*, Shatibi, *supra* note 1, at Vol. 2, p. 12 *passim*.
17. Dr. 'Abdulla, *Contemplations in Islam* p. 67 *passim*.
18. *See The Right – The Extent of the State's Authority in Restricting It* 91.
19. *Id.* at 254; Hasan Kira, *The Principles of Law* p. 44 .

The Concept of Justice and Human Rights in Islam

Noor ul-Amin Leghari[1]

INTRODUCTION

Justice is a universal value and its administration is the prime duty of the State "Justice," said Aristotle, "is the foundation of a state." Naturally, the weakness of the foundation contributes to the eventual demise of the societal structure.

Justice, in Islam, is a comprehensive concept which is not restricted to the realm of law, but permeates the society's political, economic, and social aspects as well. Since the primary focus of this paper is on its legal aspect, it will address one component of Islamic justice – the Islamic concept of human rights. To this end, the paper will compare and contrast features Islam shares with contemporary Western legal and political thought, highlighting those areas where Islam presents a unique insight. In order to consider the concept of human rights effectively, it is necessary to discuss the most important aspect of jurisprudence – justice – as Islam understands it.

The Prophet was asked, "When will justice be realized on Earth?", to which he replied, "Not until he who sees injustice being done to another suffers from the sight of it as much as its victim."[2] Similarly, 'Ali, the fourth *Caliph* of Islam said, "A country can be governed by *kufr* (heretical beliefs) for some time but with injustice not for long."[3]

The establishment of a just order in Islam requires that injustice should be exposed, ruthlessly fought, and compensation paid to its victim. Islam considers evil as real on its own plane and takes a serious view of wrongdoing. It, therefore, insists upon there being a party of people in the *Umma* who assume the duty to uphold the good and to prevent evil acts.

---

1. Professor of Islamic Jurisprudence at Sindh Muslim Law College, Karachi, Pakistan.
2. A.K. Brohi, *PLD* (1976), p. 164.
3. *Id.*

At their core, all great religions present a system of social morality along with sanctions for their transgression. As Schopenhauer used to say, "it is no doubt easy to talk about morality, but without religion you cannot make it effective." Religious sanctions, therefore, further morality.

Moral values are supreme in the sense that they are not subservient to any other value. Power is sustained only on a moral basis. Power which is acquired by resorting to immoral means cannot be maintained over time and is consequently contrary to the evolution of society. This is precisely what Plato meant when in the hierarchy of ideas he placed the idea of the good at the level representing the apex of human ideals. It is the function of *morality* to tell us what is right and proper, and it is the function of *law* to enforce such moral matters that have a direct bearing on the relationship of the individual to society. Of course if the law is secular, its enforcement is only possible on a secular basis; while if the law is religious, its enforcement is based on consequences for the afterlife as well as the present world.

The moral progress of man may be viewed as the development of rational thought. It is the rational evolution that has preceded and brought about the ethical revolution, such that intellectual development and moral development has been largely contemporaneous. Questions such as "What is the good of being good in the world" and "What can a moral man do to save himself in an immoral society?" are issues that has been pondered by a great tradition of thinkers from Tolstoy to the social and ethical philosophers of today. The answer to these questions are possible only in a *moral* sense if we concede that the claims of "humanity" represent a higher value, taking precedence over claims of the individual. The unit which must be considered in order to analyze broad questions of *morality* is the collective "humanity" and not merely the individual man or woman. Conversely, in the case of *intellectual development* it is the individual upon which attention must be directed, and it is through the individual expression that humanity as a whole is advanced.

Ethical thought *per se* has to deal with the totality of the human condition which we, as individuals, are but a part – albeit a necessary part. Once the focus of attention is shifted from the sum to its parts, to the exclusive consideration of values of a personal and individual nature, morality ceases to be true to its essence and becomes stultified and sterile.

The Greek thinkers who reached the highest pinnacle of rational thought when they were true to their ideals, invariably considered the question of right conduct in terms of justice, and their ideal was always the just man. One cannot consider a just man in the abstract, for justice, at its irreducible minimum, is a relationship of one person to another. There has to be a wider frame of reference to human relationships in which a just man may be expected to give full expression to this ideal of justice. Of course, the *Qur'an* goes much further. It considers a man unjust to himself if he is unjust to others. And this is because by inflicting injustice on others, the actor is inflicting injustice on himself, if only because he is a part of society. According to the *Qur'an*, the whole of humanity has been created *"kanafsin wahida"*, like a single indivisible self. And if you murder a man, it is as if you have murdered the whole of humanity.

The function of morality is to establish the proper relationship of the individual to the community, and the essential foundation of that relationship, based on morality, is justice. In order for an individual or a society to claim to being regarded as moral, it must cease to do wrong. The elimination of wrong is the irreducible minimum of morality.

Although the quality of mercy is a divine attribution in Islam, the emphasis on doing justice is paramount. The one concept that may be treated as a fulcrum on which the superstructure of Islam's ethical system is firmly fixed is justice. *Qur'anic* emphasis on the need to do justice in respect of *hudud* (offences) is axiomatic. In the *Qur'an*, the Prophet is asked to judge between people by means of revelation (Q.IV:105). It later goes on to say "O you who believe, be custodians of justice (and) witnesses for Allah, even though against yourselves or your parents or your relatives. Whether a man be rich or poor, Allah is his greater well-wisher than you." (Q.IV:135). The *Qur'an's* concern for justice reaches perhaps its fullest expression where it is said: "Do not spend the belongings of the orphans but for their betterment, until they come of age; and give in full measure, and weigh justly on the balance....When you say a thing, let it be just, even though the matter relates to a relative of yours, and fulfill a promise made to God" (Q.VI:152). Thus, human duties and rights have been rigorously defined and their enforcement is the collective responsibility of the community, through the legal organs of the State.

Having emphasized the supreme importance of the concept of justice, the task of enforcing justice acquires primacy, and human rights are only one aspect of the large and liberal concept of justice in this context.

HUMAN RIGHTS: HISTORICAL BACKGROUND

Man, by nature, is a social animal. His nature compels him to live among his fellow beings. From cradle to grave, he depends on the services, care, and attention of others. He is forced to live in a social environment, not only to fulfill his basic needs, but also for the development and application of his natural capabilities. This, in turn, gives rise to a host of relationships that he establishes around himself. These relationships range from domestic life to international relations. The question of rights and obligations is but a natural corollary of the social network within which he operates. In various capacities, he accepts certain obligations which, in turn, entitle him to certain rights.

Some of these are moral rights such as the right of the elders to be respected, the young ones to be loved, and the needy to receive assistance. Others are juridical rights, such as property rights and the right of compensation for civil damages. These latter rights are recognized by law and protected through courts as legal or positive rights.

There is yet another aspect of man's rights which is related to his interaction with the State. The rights that he enjoys against the State are referred to as "fundamental rights", which implies that such rights are protected by the constitution and that no organ of the State, whether legislative, executive, or judicial, shall violate them. These rights are conferred on the individual, not only in his capacity as a citizen of the State, but also on the basis of his inclusion in the universal brotherhood of mankind. No distinction is, therefore, made on the basis of color, race, ethnicity, religion, or language.

The basic objective of enshrining human rights in the constitution is to define the scope of State powers so that a ruler may not deprive individuals of their rights and assume dictatorial powers. With fundamental rights guaranteed, an individual is provided with the opportunity to realize his/her fullest potential without undue interference from other members of society or the ruling authority.

Although the concept of human rights is a historical tradition which was known to poets, philosophers, and politicians in antiquity and the Middle Ages, it gradually assumed its present prominence in the West in the context of a thousand years of European history and development. The evil effects of civil wars, autocracy, feudal exploitation, excessive dominance of the Church, religious wars, and racial nationalism rendered an individual helpless before the State which continued to expand its power at his expense. This set the stage for thinking men to espouse the cause of human rights by recommending effective checks of the powers of the State. We see this manifested in the writings of political thinkers during the Renaissance, later finding expression in the American and French constitutions. After the horrors of the two World Wars, the need for the promotion and protection of human rights assumed a universal and international character, through the United Nation's "Declaration of Universal Human Rights" and various other legal instruments.

In Islam, the concept of human rights did not originate or develop through historical experience. Man was endowed with these rights by the Creator at the time of his creation. He was given a code of social conduct which contained a clear concept of rights and obligations. Therefore, the first man to inhabit the planet, according to the *Qur'an*, knew very well the real purpose of his creation. "And God gave Adam knowledge of the nature and reality of all things..." (Q.II:31).

The dispute between the two sons of Adam, Abel and Cain, regarding the acceptance of their respective sacrifices by Allah is narrated in the *Qur'an*.

> Narrate to them exactly the tale of the two sons of Adam. When each of them offered a sacrifice to (to God), that of one was accepted, and that of the other was not. Said (the one): "I will murder you," and the other replied: "God only accepts from those who are upright and preserve themselves from evil. If you raise your hand to kill me, I will not raise mine to kill you, for I fear God, the Lord of all worlds; I

would rather you suffered the punishment for sinning against me, and for your own sin, and became an inmate of Hell. And that is the requital for the unjust" (Q.V:28-30).

This indicates that Abel had a clear conception of right from wrong, and knew that taking the life of a person was a grave sin and injustice. Therefore, being a righteous person, he preferred to lay down his life rather than violate the sanctity of human life.

The divine guidance conveyed through the chain of prophets to different peoples in different eras was not confined to the realm of beliefs but encompassed other aspects of life as well. Regarding Moses, the *Qur'an* states, "And We wrote down on tablets admonitions and clear explanations of all things for Moses, and ordered him: "Hold fast to them, and command your people to observe the best in them...."(Q.VII:145).

Speaking in specific terms of rights and obligations, the *Qur'an* narrates the outlines given to the children of Israel through Moses: "Remember, where We made a covenant with the people of Israel and said: 'Worship no one but God, and be good to your parents and kin, and to orphans and the needy, and speak of goodness to men; observe your devotional duties and give *zakat* (the due share of your wealth for the welfare of others)'....And remember, when we made a covenant with you whereby you agreed you will neither shed blood among you nor turn your people out of their homes...."(Q.II:83-84).

The Prophet Muhammad's best treatment of the issue of fundamental rights was in his final sermon, on the occasion of his last pilgrimage to Makka. The resonance of human rights, therefore, is discernable in all the Prophet's teachings.

The history of human rights, from the Islamic perspective, leads one to perceive that they are coeval with man. They emanate from the divine will and not from the State or any other sovereign; hence, they are inalienable and irrevocable under all circumstances. Consequently, the function of the State is not to *determine* but to *protect and enforce* them.

Legal Perspectives on Human Rights

In considering the issue of human rights from a legal perspective, Islam presents a viewpoint that is distinct on the following grounds:

Divine source

The prevalent model of human rights primarily focuses its attention on regulating the relationship of an individual with the State though a recognition of certain fundamental rights which the former enjoys and the latter undertakes not to violate. These rights, by their very nature, are defensive and protective. When they are enshrined in a constitution, the State, as a sovereign, concedes these rights, while the individual, as the weaker party, is their recipient. The individual and the State are thus defined relationally by the constitution as a compromissory document.

The Islamic model of human rights represents a different hierarchy. Since sovereignty in Islam belongs to Almighty Allah, fundamental rights emanate from Him. The individual and the State are not parties with competing interests but are coexistent recipients of divine injunctions. The State has neither the unilateral authority to award these rights nor the jurisdiction to abrogate, amend, or suspend them. Therefore, they are irrevocable and inalienable under all circumstances.

Scope of fundamental rights

As a logical corollary of the divine source of Islamic law, the scope of fundamental rights widens to include all rights ordained by the *Shari'a* whether they fall under the conventional definition of fundamental rights or not. Current Islamic thought tends to conclude that there is no reason why the scope of fundamental rights should be restricted to such rights as the rights of life, honor, property, justice, equality, freedom of expression, assembly, and religious practice without also encompassing all rights which have been enjoined by the Supreme Law Giver and are therefore irrevocable and enforceable by the courts. The following examples illustrate this point.

The *Qur'an* specifies the right of a new born baby to be suckled for two years (Q.II:233) and lays down the rights and obligations of the parents in this regard. During the lifetime of the Prophet, a pregnant woman confessed to committing adultery and pleaded that the requisite punishment – the death penalty – be awarded to her. The Prophet asked her to come back after giving birth to her child. She did so, but the Prophet sent her back again and asked her to compete the period of breast feeding. She complied with the orders and thereafter due punishment was given to her. In this particular instance, if the punishment had been awarded at the time of the confession of the crime, the child's right to life would have been violated, and if the punishment had not been postponed for the second time, his right to survival would have been jeopardized. The Prophet suspended the execution of the punishment until the realization of the two fundamental rights. Since the right of a child to be suckled is laid down in the *Qur'an*, it was treated on par with another universally recognized fundamental right, the right to life.

The second example relates to the issue of the marital gift (dower) given by a man to his wife at the time of their marriage. The *Qur'an* states: "Give to women their dowers willingly, but if they forego part of it themselves, then use it to your advantage" (Q.IV:4). Thus, enjoined by Allah, the right to receive the dower became a fundamental right of the woman. During the reign of the second *Caliph* 'Umar, some restrictions were proposed on the application of this right. During one of his sermons, a woman stood up and challenged 'Umar's right to restrict or nullify a right through legislation which had been specifically set forth in the *Qur'an*. 'Umar, upon realizing his mistake, withdrew his decision.[4]

The same principle can be extended to all other rights and obligations that are specifically set forth in the *Qur'an* or Traditions of the Prophet. The scope of fundamental rights in Islam, therefore, is not limited to those areas that have a direct bearing on the relationship of an individual to the State, but also includes those rights that regulate his or her relations with other individuals. Thus, the nature of human rights in Islam is not only defensive and protective against a coercive State, but assumes a positive character as well.

Enforcement Mechanisms

The enforcement of fundamental human rights is another area where a brief treatment of Islamic methodology may prove instructive.

Modern constitutions are generally regarded as documentary guardians of fundamental human rights and the enforcement of their protections is ensured through the courts of law. Although this system has worked reasonably well in the West, this model has been far from satisfactory in the developing world where constitutions have been frequently subject to amendment, suspension, and abrogation. In the absence of a mature political culture, democratic traditions, and social awareness, constitutions have not proven to be an effective instrument of control over ruling authorities. Legislatures are subject to pressure from political parties and, depending on the constitutional tradition, the courts may be rendered ineffective by legislatures that have the power to restrict their review jurisdiction.

Even in some advanced countries, legislatures often have the power to give sweeping powers to their governments in times of war and national emergencies, which adversely impacts the fundamental rights of the people. In Great Britain, for example, Parliament passed the "Defence of the Realm Act" during the First World War, and the "Emergency Power Defence Act" during the Second World War which gave extremely broad powers to the wartime governments in matters relating to the economy and national defense.

The American constitutional structure is unique in that it allows the Supreme Court to review any legislation passed by Congress and declare it unconstitutional.[5] Nevertheless, in the case of rebellion or invasion, the Constitu-

---

4. M. Hamidullah, *Khutbat Bahawalpur* (Islamabad), p. 98.
5. *See* Marbury v. Madison, 5 U.S. (1 Cranch.) 137 (1803).

tion provides for the suspension of the writ of Habeas Corpus.⁶ It remains undeniable that over the past two centuries, the individual has fared better in the developed world than in any other region. This is partly because of constitutional protections of the individual enforced through the judiciary, but primarily because of a long tradition of constitutionalism that became entrenched in these societies as a result of relative stability over time.

Dorothy Pickles, commenting on this issue, observes that:

> The only ultimate safe-guard of constitutionality would seem to be the practice of it over a long period of time, and circumstances do not always permit this. Invasion, defeat in war, deep-seated and irreconcilable divisions within a country – these can make the normal development of constitutional government very difficult, and even impossible. The United States and Great Britain have both been fortunate in that they have enjoyed long periods of comparative invulnerability from external aggression and have been relatively free from the internal instability.[7]

In countries where the threat of external aggression or internal instability has been a recurring phenomenon, the constitution and judiciary have not proved to be effective instruments for the preservation of fundamental human rights.

The enforcement of rights and their ultimate preservation in Islam, on the other hand, must be considered in light of Allah's sovereignty which is the core principle of Muslim polity. The ultimate authority within the community, whether legislative, executive, or judicial, is exercisable by the believers by virtue of their covenant with Allah, and with due regard for the priorities established by Him. The ruling instrumentalities are equally bound to follow the divine command as their subjects are. Since rights and obligations emanate from the ultimate Sovereign, they cannot be revoked or suspended by the State, even in the face of external or internal exigencies.

The *Caliph* Abu Bakr's sermon for the guidance of soldiers who were then engaged in war on the Syrian front is quite illuminating in this regard. He says,

> Be just, break not your plighted faith, mutilate none, slay neither children, old men, nor women; injure not the date-palm nor burn it with fire, nor cut down any fruit-bearing tree, slay neither flocks nor herds nor camels except for food, perchance you may come across men who have retired into monasteries, leave them and their work in peace.[8]

By extension, under strict Islamic legal theory, there cannot be a conflict

---

6. U.S. CONST. art. I, §2, cl. 2.
7. Dorothy Pickles, *Democracy* (London, 1960), p. 133.
8. Brohi, *supra* note 1, at 153.

between State authority and the individual, since both are subject to the same divine will.

MORAL ASPECTS OF RIGHTS

After considering the question of rights from both historical and legal perspectives, it is instructive to consider their moral implications as well. Two points need to be analyzed in this regard:

Moral duties contrasted with legal obligations

There are certain rights which fall under the jurisdiction of the courts of law and are enforced by the State. These legal rights are expressed in positive law and include such rights as the right to life, property rights, and the freedoms of expression and assembly, *inter alia*. On the other hand, the right of the poor to receive assistance, the rights of parents to be cared for, and respect for neighbors are examples of moral rights which lack the enforcement power of the State.

As far as legal rights are concerned, both Islamic and secular laws provide a legal mechanism for their enforcement. By contrast, the secular world may provide a moral framework of right and wrong, but leaves its implementation to individual volition. The only external force which may provide a motivation for compliance is communal pressure which, although persuasive, fails to ensure a desirable level of commitment. The implementation of moral rights in an Islamic society achieves a greater prominence because of the sacred and religious nature of Islamic law. Since the ultimate source of both legal and moral rights in Islam is the same, the religious consciousness of the believer provides him with a forceful incentive to fulfill his moral obligations, even in the absence of societal pressure.

Impact of the human character

The question of compliance with legal rights must also be viewed in a broader context. The Western model seems to imply that mechanical conformity to legally prescribed rules of conduct will suffice to secure public order and universal peace. In other words, its seeks to apply external influence to the internal condition of man, in the belief that its institutions, whether social, economic, or political, have a way of influencing individual character. Islam, on the other hand, begins by inviting man to accept the supremacy of the power of the Lord, thereby becoming subservient to the will of the Master who is the sovereign ruler of the universe. It further redeems him by prescribing norms of behavior with which to regulate life. Consequently, Islam seeks to influence the external conditions of man by focusing on the internal, without underestimating the influence of political, economic, and social institutions on the human character.

To maximize the observance of human rights, or any other legal norm for that matter, Islam gives due regard for the inner as well as outer dimensions of the human personality. A mere reliance on external sources may not secure the desired objectives. Modern behavioral science also recognizes the importance of this duality. Professor Zbigniew Brzezinski observes that:

> One can call the foregoing 'procedural morality', based on external rules guiding conduct and social interaction. It differs fundamentally from a morality that is internalized, personal and inclined to make a distinction between 'right' and 'wrong'...under ideal circumstances in a law respecting democracy, procedural morality and inner morality would be mutually reinforcing.... In the past, that latter role was largely played by organized religion. But in modern society both politics and economics conspire to create a culture inimical to the preservation of an important social domain reserved for the religious. An increasingly permissive culture, exploiting the principle of the separation of church and state, squeezes out the religious factor but without substituting for it any secular 'categorical imperative', thereby transforming the inner moral code into a vacuum.[9]

Islam perhaps can help to fill this vacuum which is gradually assuming a global proportion and may eventually disrupt the legal, social, and political fabric of our society.

Enforcement of Human Rights

In order to maximize the applicability of rights, Islam not only presents a "Charter of Human Rights" as exemplified by the last sermon of the Prophet, but also emphasizes personal accountability, which represents a duty owed by the individual to Allah. Given that Allah is the fountainhead of all sovereignty, every believer knows that even if he disobeys the order of a secular authority and escapes earthly punishment, he will eventually account for it on the Day of Judgment, particularly where his misdeeds have harmed others. Thus, one might conclude that man as such has no rights but only duties toward his Maker within a theocentric construct where Allah, the only reality, is in the center. However, these duties in turn give rise to all forms of rights, including human rights in the contemporary sense of the term. The *Qur'an* is full of guidelines

---

9. Zbigniew Brzezinski, *Out of Control: Global Turmoil on the Eve of the Twenty-first Century* (Scribner, New York 1993), pp. 67-68.

with which a believer is expected to act in conformity. The following verses from Chapter 17 illustrate this point:

> So your Lord has decreed: Do not worship anyone but Him, and be good to your parents. If one or both of them grow old in your presence, do not say fie to them, nor reprove them, but say gentle words to them... (Q.XVII:23)
>
> So give to relatives what is their due, and to those who are needy, and the wayfarers; and do not dissipate (your wealth) extravagantly (Q.XVII:26).
>
> And do not go near fornication, as it is immoral and an evil way (Q.XVII:32).
>
> And do not take a life, which God has forbidden, except in a just cause. We have given the right (of redress) to the heir of the person who is killed, but he should not exceed the limits of (justice) by slaying (the killer), for he will be judged (by the same law) (Q.XVII:33).
>
> And do not touch the property of the orphans except for bettering it, until they come of age; and fulfil the promise made: You will surely be questioned about the promise.(Q.XVII:34).
>
> Give full measure when you are measuring, and weigh on a balanced scale. This is better and excellent its consequence (Q.XVII:35).
>
> This is some of the wisdom your Lord has revealed to you. So do not take another god apart from God, or you will be cast into Hell, reproved, ostracized (Q.XVII:39).

The *Qur'anic* insistence on fulfilling one's responsibilities does not necessarily entail undermining the importance of one's rights. Rather, both may be viewed as mutually reinforcing. Undue insistence on one at the cost of the other very often upsets the delicate balance so necessary in social morality. Our dilemma in the modern age is that we have lost sight of the importance of the relationship between rights and obligations. As Edmund Burke observed in 1791, "Men are qualified for civil liberty in exact proportion to their own appetites."[10] Professor Brzezinski similarly notes that "In a society that culturally emphasizes the maximization of moral restraints, civic freedom tends to be elevated into a self-validating absolute. In other words, civic freedom is divorced from a notion of civic responsibility."[11]

Today, respect for human rights all over the world is far from satisfactory. This cannot be ensured merely by enshrining them in national and international legal instruments. This requires a change in attitude and a moral framework that puts one's obligations on an equal footing with one's rights. Perhaps

---

10. Edmund Burke, *quoted in* Richard M. Nixon, *Beyond Peace* (Random House, New York 1993) p. 236.
11. Brzezinski, *supra* note 7, at 69.

the world needs a "Universal Declaration of Human Obligations" as a counterpart to the "Universal Declaration of Human Rights" that we have had for almost half a century.

In addition to instilling a sense of accountability in the individual, Islam places a great deal of emphasis on the rule of law as a means of obligating public authorities to safeguard human rights. Their power to govern is subject to the following constitutional limitations:

Equality of ruler and subject before the law

Like any other individual, the ruler is bound by the *Shari'a* in personal as well as public conduct. This is because of the fundamental principle of Islam that Allah is the ultimate sovereign, and the ruler, as his trustee, is entrusted only to run the affairs of the people. Thus, the ruler represents a person with a larger share of obligations than an ordinary member of the community. The very manner of exercising public power under Islamic law assumes the absence of any special status which would place the ruler apart from the ruled.

There are many historical precedents which support this view. For example, Abu Bakr, in his inaugural speech as the first *Caliph*, declared:

> O, people, I have been made the ruler amongst you, and I am not the best of you. So if I act rightly, help me, and if I am in error, correct me....The weak amongst you is strong in my eyes till I bring, with the help of Allah, to him what is his right. And the strongest amongst you is weak (in my eyes) till I take from him with the help of Allah, what is due....[12]

***Ultra vires* acts of the ruler**

The second constitutional restraint relates to the limits of obedience due to a ruler. The *Qur'an* is replete with verses that illustrate that obedience to the ruler is mandatory only where the law is itself lawful, and that the ruler should not be obeyed if doing so would involve disobedience to Allah. The *Qur'an* states: "But help one another in goodness and piety, and do not assist in crime and rebellion, and fear God"(Q.V:2). The Prophet is reported to have said, "Listening and obeying is obligatory on every Muslim, male or female, in what he likes or dislikes so long as he is not ordered to disobey [Allah]; but when he is ordered to disobey [Allah] then there is no listening and obeying."[13]

---

12. Khalid M. Ishaque, *Constitutional Limitations* (Pakistan Publishing House., Karachi 1972), p. 10.

Judicial review

These two principles, the equality of the ruler and the ruled under the *Shari'a*, and the unenforceability of *ultra vires* commands of the ruler, taken together, lead to a third constitutional restraint – the right of the people to demand judicial review of the enforceability of a command between the ruler and the ruled. The ruler, being bound by the *Shari'a*, is subject to its jurisdiction as is any other member of the community. Any person who claims that his words are the law, without there being any person or body having authority to adjudicate the validity of his command, usurps a right which Allah has not conferred on him.

On the contrary, Allah says, "O you who believe, obey God and the Prophet and those in authority among you; and if you are in variance over something, refer it to God and the Messenger, if you believe in God and the Last Day. This is good for you and the best of settlements" (Q.IV:59). This verse clearly contemplates that disputes may arise among members of the community, and between the rulers and the ruled, and that such disputes should be resolved on the basis of guidelines set forth by Allah and His Prophet. Therefore, no ruling body can lawfully deny a person the right to seek judicial redress in a dispute with the state, nor can any court of law declare a law to be valid which purports to abrogate this right.

We have already noted Abu Bakr's statement recognizing the limits of his authority. During the last days of 'Uthman's *caliphate*, a number of persons came to Madina and repeatedly pressed him to account for some of his public dealings. Even if the *Caliph* was convinced that they were wrong, he did not deprive them of their right to demand an explanation from him. Similarly, when Mu'awiya raised the issue of the failure of 'Ali to punish the murderers of 'Uthman, it was referred to arbitration. 'Ali's willingness to agree to arbitral review demonstrated his recognition of the right to judicially challenge the *Caliph's* public conduct. Other instances may be noted, including the appearance of the *Caliphs* 'Umar and 'Ali before the court to explain their public and private conduct. It may therefore be argued that the tradition of judicial review of all actions in the public and private sectors is inherent in the Islamic sociopolitical order.

Public consultation

A final form of constitutional restraint placed on the public authorities by the *Shari'a* is the exercise of power on the basis of public consultation. The

---

13. *Mishkat*, Vol. 2, p. 317.

form and method of such consultation is not specified, and therefore varies according to circumstances and exigencies. The *Qur'an*, in reference to believers, ordains that, "[Allah's reward is better and more enduring for those] who obey the commands of their Lord and...whose affairs are settled by mutual consultation" (Q.ILII:38). In the absence of a revelation, even the Prophet has been asked to follow the same principle. "[A]nd seek their counsel in all affairs" (Q.III:159).

The fourth *Caliph* 'Ali, expounding on the principle of consultation, narrates the following discourse he had with the Prophet:

> I said, O Prophet of Allah, if a situation arises after you, about which there us no specific guidance in the *Qur'an* or in your own traditions, [what should we do in such a situation]? He said, "Gather the righteous learned people in my *Umma*, consult them and do not decide the matter on the opinion of one person."[14]

No Muslim ruler, given the above *Qur'anic* and prophetic injunctions, can justify discharging his public responsibilities arbitrarily, without seeking the participation of the people in the process. The duty to consult is in relation to the community as a whole and is always subject to the community's right to question, criticize, and guide the ruling agencies. Therefore, whenever the community has agreed to a form of consultation and has selected persons to act as their representatives, the ruling authority may not bypass such a body, even in the name of national emergencies, which arise with amazing frequency whenever a ruler attempts to exceed his lawful authority.

CONCLUSION

Within the confines of a short paper such as this, it is not possible to consider all aspects of so vast a subject as human rights. However, it is hoped that the foregoing discussion has helped to reinforce that Islam not only considers respect for human rights to be fundamental to its own concept of justice but may in fact offer means through which the cause of human rights may be advanced globally, beyond their currently deplorable level of observance.

There is no denying that there is a gap between theory and practice in the Muslim world, but this phenomenon is by no means confined to it, cutting across all regions and social structures. To bridge this divergence between idealism and reality is the challenge facing the world today, and the potential role that Islam might play in this regard must be judged on the intrinsic value of its ideal and not by the present practice of its adherents.

---

14. Maudoodi, Syed Abul Maududi, *First Principles of the Islamic State* (Urdu edition, Lahore), p. 373 .

The Concept of Justice in Islamic Jurisprudence

Ali Bardakoglu[1]

The Islamic concept of justice is a multi-dimensional concept which has different shades of meaning in different disciplines. Therefore, the term "justice" has different scope and definitions, corresponding to usages in linguistics, the *Qur'an, hadith*, Islamic law *(Shar'ia)*, theology *(kalam)*, ethics, and Islamic philosophy; or in accordance with such traditions as politics, administration, and the organisation and practice of Muslim societies.

The *Qur'an* mentions the term "*'adl*" twenty eight times, "*Qist*" twenty five times, and "*haqq*" or its roots some three hundred times. These terms as used in the *Qur'an* represent concepts such as order, balance, equality, honesty, equity, and passing proper judgment, which are in fact similar to each other and express the values of justice found in the nature of human beings. Islamic society is defined in the *Qur'an* as being balanced, coherent and just (Q.II:143; Q.XVII:29; Q.XXV:63, 67-68; Q.XLVIII:29). In the *Qur'an* someone who lacks the characteristics of justice is compared to a slave who is dumb, helpless, and useless. Moreover, the *Qur'an* states that such a person cannot be deemed equal to someone who has the virtue of justice and follows the "straight path" (Q.XVI:76). To be able to obtain the virtue of piety, which is the highest attainment, one must be just (Q.V:8; Q.VI:152). Loyalty and justice *(adl)* are among the characteristics of divine revelations (Q.VI:115).

According to the *Qur'an*, the criteria for justice is fairness and equity. Divine blessing is obtained through the practice of justness and the observance of equity (Q.VII:159, 181). The *Qur'an* has established criteria for justness. For example, the *Qur'an's* revelations consider an act to be oppression when justness is observed by nations only when it is to their advantage (Q.XXIV:48-51). Moreover, the failure to observe justice, owing to emotional factors such as personal favour, enmity, and discrimination on the grounds of race, colour,

---

[1]. Dr. Ali Bardakoglu is Professor of Islamic Law and Jurisprudence at The Faculty of Theology, The Marmara University, in Istanbul.

and creed are strongly condemned in the *Qur'an* (Q.III:75; Q.IV:3; Q.V:8). All human acts, both in this world and the hereafter, will be judged by Allah on the basis of justice (Q.X:54-55; Q.XXI:47; Q.XXXIX:69; Q.XCIX:7-8).

However, it is also stated that humans have frailties, consequently perfect justice is not realizable. Therefore, the *Qur'an* pragmatically acknowledges that it would be enough to make an effort to be just (Q.IV:129). In fact, according to Islamic belief, the only absolute justice is divine justice which will be realized in the hereafter. Allah alone is absolutely just. Consequently, Islam does not seek to establish absolute justice in this world. Both general principles derived from the *Qur'an*, and the *Qur'an's* specific judgments, are concrete forms of divine justice, in accordance with people and their society. These are not restrictions on the lives and freedoms of human beings. On the contrary, they are meant to help human beings by giving them some insight into divine justice and to guide them on the right way, while protecting them from subjective justice. For this reason, Islamic scholars treat Allah's judgments on individuals and social life as falling within the context of Allah's blessing. Human beings, despite all unfavourable circumstances, are able to establish the most just and lawfully ordered lifestyle for themselves by living according to the principles and guidance given by Allah.

Justice is not defined in the *Qur'an*, although it is frequently mentioned, and Muslims are ordered to be just in the *Qur'an* and *hadith*. Consequently, the definition of justice is obtainable in part within the logic and circumstances of each incident. The *Qur'an*, by not giving a definition, implies its confidence in the people who believe in Allah and the day of judgment. Furthermore, Allah implies his confidence in responsible, mature people as to their ability to observe justice in every incident and circumstance. In the observation of justice, both individually and socially, the human factor and personal ability of those implementing law bear more importance than the law to be implemented.

Justice, according to Islamic law, is the aim of humanity. But the *nature* of justice has always been debatable. According to Islamic jurisprudence, there are two types of justice. One is based on reason. This form of justice, like other concepts based on reason, is general and abstract. It is often called *husn* and its opposite is called *Qubh*. These principles, such as the obligations not to harm anyone, to return kindness with kindness, and to give to another what he or she deserves, are examples of this kind of justice. The second one is justice based on laws and rules. It is more specific, changeable, and casual in comparison to the former. Current laws in force are not determinative of what is justice. It is the first kind of justice that gives legitimacy to the laws in force. Since law is a normative science, it brings forward ideals, not realities. The order of law is a means to have an order of social life, aiming to establish justice. That judicial decisions and criteria are principally mentioned in the *Qur'an* and *hadith* aims to establish a coherent communication between lawful justice and judicial justice.

The Islamic concept of justice is in harmony with the modern concept which divides justice into objective and subjective elements. It is true that there are objective and subjective appearances of justice.[2] Justice, as an individual virtue, has a subjective nature. Everybody generally presumes that he or she intends to be good, right, and just. But this *presumption* and effort is itself *subjective justice*. In other words, this is a *stand* for justice, not justice *itself*. However, apart from individual presumptions and values inspired by community, there is an idea of equity and justice, which, as ethical values, are hidden in human nature. The improvement of positive law can be achieved through the exercise of these supreme values. Law is often defined in terms of the values of justice contained in it. But objective justice is known only in the form of judgments made in concrete incidents.

In studies on modern law and jurisprudence, although special attention has been given to objective justice, not enough efforts have yet been taken to reduce the elements of subjective justice. To achieve objective justice and set out the values of justice hidden in the human being depends on asserting the type of mental values that would protect men from the impact of unfavourable circumstances. This, in turn, will depend on providing a good education, strong and responsible personality, and ethical maturity. Islam, by considering some rules as religious, ethical and judicial values, aims at establishing a common ground to protect human intellect from the impact of continuing change. In other words, justice in Islam is not merely an idea or value of law, but also a religious and ethical value as well. Although law generally depends on ethics, in Islam it is *religion* which protects ethics from relativity and unfavourable influences. It is exceedingly difficult to keep basic values alive without religion and faith.

This does not mean that in Islam legislation will be provided by the clergy, or that society will be governed in accordance with justice established by them, on behalf of Allah. Theocracy is contrary to the concept of justice and law. Today, in Islamic lands, positive law is made free from the religious establishments. What Islam stresses is the establishment of a coherent relationship among religion, ethics and law to achieve justice. In the West, steps have been taken to protect the legislative, executive, and judicial functions of the government from the pressures of the Church and the clergy, to assert their religious and ethical norms on legislation. It is only through a coherent co-operation among these three fields that an objective justice, distinct from the subjective form could be achieved. The general outline of the concept of justice in the *Qur'an, sunna*, and jurisprudence, has asserted a special meaning in the understanding of the concepts of natural law, equity (*istihsan*) and the consideration of public interest (*istislah*). In this paper we shall examine the concept of justice in Islam in light of these three concepts.

---

2. The division of substantive justice and procedural justice made by Khadduri, provides another perspective on the theory and practice of justice. *See* Majid Khadduri, *The Islamic Concept of Justice*, (Baltimore 1984), pp. 135-49.

THE CONCEPT OF NATURAL LAW

Today, some jurists argue that the theological law that replaced the classical natural law in the middle ages, denied it the right to exist, and diminished the dualism of "positive law-natural law" and that theological law representing a narrow conception of law was acceptable only to its believers, contrary to the universality of natural law. Thus, they claim that theological law delayed the development of natural law in the middle ages.[3] It is perhaps necessary to say that differences between the Western and Islamic concepts of divine law have existed ever since Islam came into existence.

The established principles of Islamic law and its sources are basically permanent, not dependent on time or changing circumstances. Thus, the divinely-originated judgments and principles mandated by Islamic law are dogmatic in nature. These principles are considered ideals for Muslims and perfect models for other rules and laws of positive law. Human beings, guided by these models, must then adhere as closely as possible to their underlying principles. It is natural that we do not find such a division as "reality ideal" regarding judgments derived from divine will. This is because the fact that such judgments are divinely originated creates the belief that these are the best and most just laws. However, the issue of *"husn"* and *"qubh"* discussed both in *Kalam* (theology) and Islamic jurisprudence, is partly related to this matter.

Moreover, both the general principles and particular private judgments of the *Qur'an* and the *sunna* (traditions) are never considered inconsistent with universal principles of reason. General principles are of necessity derived from universal experience. Particular judgments were arrived at either to satisfy a specific matter or to establish a specific principle. Thus, the principles derived from these two sources of law may be synthesized into a unified form. For example, the *Qur'an* states: "O believers, you should not usurp unjustly the wealth of each other, but trade by mutual consent; and do not destroy yourselves. God is merciful to you"(Q.IV:29), "Verily God has enjoined justice, the doing of good, and the giving of gifts to your relatives; and forbidden indecency, impropriety and oppression. He warns you so that you may remember" (Q.XVI :90), "O you who believe, fulfil your obligations" (Q.V:l). The *sunna* also states: "it is illegal both to give harm, and to respond to harm with harm."[4] These and other similar judgments, along with common sense principles, represent the foundations upon which positive law in Islam is framed.

Perhaps the most striking aspect is that the understanding, interpretation, and implementation of these principles are left to human beings. As a practical matter, the determination of the parameters of these principles, and decisions

---

3. Tar k Özbilgen, *Tabii Hukuk Görüsünden Sosyolojik Hukuk Görüsüne* (Istanbul Üniversitesi Hukuk Fakültesi Mecmuasi), Vol. 30, no. 1-2, pp. 8-11.

4. Malik b. Anas, *al-Muwatta* (Cairo 1951), Vol. 2, p. 22 .

regarding the implementation and practice of such principles as justice, injustice, and *pacta sunt servanda* are entrusted to human beings in each era and the consequent results depended on their sensitivity. Thus, not only is it beyond question that the principles of divine law are contrary to the ideals of natural law, but also it cannot be argued that divine law superseded natural law. On the contrary, it can be argued that the ideal law, hidden in the endless depths of the human spirit, although illuminated by divine law, finds expression in the form of the principles of positive law. Moreover, the acceptance of the general principles of religion may be explained by the fact that they are in conformity with human ideals and with common sense. Some Islamic theologians may have wished to emphasize this point when they were searching for *husn* and *kubh* as distinct from the divine will.

It may be asserted that the principles of natural law, as developed throughout the ages, forming the basis of legal thought in the Western world, is in harmony with the general principles of Islamic religion. For example, consider the term "justice", one of the basic concepts of natural law, which was defined by Hugo Grotius (1583-1645) in such terms as "not to harm any one", to "give everyone what he or she is owed", "respect for rights", "equal punishment for equal crime", and "*pacta sunt servanda*". In the 18th century, Thomassus defined justice as the basis of three stages of moral development: (1) "do not respond with the thing which you do not want for yourself"; (2) "do the thing for yourself which you wish others to do for you"; and (3) "do to others the thing you wish others do to you".[5] All such principles have been recognized by the *Qur'an* and traditions at a much earlier time during the tenth and eleventh centuries. Similarly, Islam recognized positive law principles of natural law prior to Western recognition. Both Grotius and Thomassus were known for their efforts to secularize natural law by separating it from religion and ethics.[6]

Reason has been regarded as one of the five necessities of life, worthy of protection, and any action harmful to reason has been prohibited in the Islamic faith.[7] It is taken for granted that the principles and the philosophy of natural law were not considered contrary to the spirit of Islam. Commentators who often asserted that the principles derived from divine sources that contradict universal ideals of law are often mislead, possibly because either the prin-

---

5. M. Niyazi Öktem, *Hukuk Felsefesi* (Istanbul 1983), pp. 62-63.

6. It was not until the sixteenth and seventeenth centuries that Europe produced the ideological basis for political legitimacy independent of religious institutions. Consequently this wave of secularist thought was, at least initially, in reaction to the pervasive power of the Church, rather than in opposition to the general principles and values of Christianity.

7. Ibn Amir al-Haj, *al-Taqrir wa al-Tahrir* (Bulaq 1316), Vol. 3, p. 144; *see also* Nizam al-Din 'Abd al-Hamid, *Tatawwur al-Fikr al-Islami wa Masadir al-'Aqliya*, in *Kulliyat al-Shari'a*, (Baghdad 1981),Vol. 7, pp. 127-128.

ciples of religion are not clearly understood, or the principles of natural law were perceived incorrectly.

Because Islamic law has been expounded and systematized by the schools of law, many researchers have incorrectly concluded that Islamic law, based on the divine will, is formalistically of an untouchable and unchangeable nature. However, in reality the superb efforts made by Muslim jurists was only to understand and interpret the textual sources of Islamic law and solve social problems in the light of such textual sources. Those who view Islamic law as static are mistaken, as they are not careful to differentiate divine sources from sources based on reason.

Muslim jurists who did not see in the textual sources of Islamic law a basis for positive law to be derived from the ideal law point of view, instead recognized the division of "reality-ideal" in the process of making judgments on the basis of reasonable deduction from the *Qur'an* and *sunna* (traditions) on all matters where there is no explicit basis in these two sources. This may be seen as a different approach to the bifurcation of justice into objective and subjective components. But this dualistic approach to Islamic law raises the question as to whether judicial judgments, formed within a methodological context, which stressed a positive content, are necessarily ideal results, or, in other words, whether the given result in a particular case is in harmony with the spirit of Islam. The theories created by the schools of Islamic law, and the toleration observed by the various schools has been an important factor in sustaining the developments in this direction. Thus, the division between "reality-ideal" has appeared, not in the textual sources of Islam, but in the opinions and independent judgment of Muslim jurists who interpreted and updated the textual sources. The primary sources of authority in this context are obviously the general principles of the Islam as mandated by the *Qur'an* and *sunna*. The general concept of justice is considered the essence of the *Qur'an* and *sunna*. The clearest basis of this theory are the concepts of *istihsan* and *istislah* to which Muslim jurists have resorted.

ISTIHSAN (EQUITY OR JURISTIC PREFERENCE)

The need for responding to the new challenges facing Muslim societies in the first and early second centuries of the Islamic State led Muslim jurists to interpret the *Qur'an* and *sunna* through opinion (*ra'i*) and the precedent set by the early *Caliphs* who succeeded the Prophet. The schools of law, which began to develop from the latter part of the second century of Islam established a certain procedure of analogy to legitimize the practice of judgment by opinion, which although widespread, was severely criticized for its lack of rules and predictability. The practice of reasoning by analogy, apart from the reasoning of a decision based on religious texts, established a valid decision for an otherwise similar situation which was not contemplated in the textual sources.⁸ However, since analogy was subject to criticism because it was not always consistent with the principles of Islamic jurisprudence, a more liberal methodology was developed by the *hanafi* school, called "*istihsan.*" The word "*istihsan*" is derived from the Arabic root-letters "*h-s-n*", and literally means "to deem something nice and good". It is often translated into English as "approval,"⁹ "preference,"¹⁰ "unreasoned preference,"¹¹ juristic preference or equity.¹² There are many definitions of *istihsan*. For example, al-Karkhi (d. 340/951) a *Hanafi* jurist, defines *istihsan* as "departing to another judgment from similar judgments in a problem, because of some other more powerful reasons," while Pazdawi (d.483/1090) views it as "inclining to a more powerful analogy than judgment laid by an analogy."¹³ Al-Sarakhsi (d.483/1090) describes *istihsan* as "embracing the best alternative for people, acting in accordance with easiness, tolerance and permission,"¹⁴ or "to accept the proof which is contradictory with open analogy and is more powerful than that."¹⁵ Other schools define *istihsan* in similar terms.¹⁶

Taken together, a reasonably useful synthesis of these conceptualization of *istihsan* would state that "*istihsan* is to depart from a judgment based on *Shar'ia* proof, by means of a second, more powerful *Shar'ia* proof." In another words, it legitimizes a judgment which is otherwise contrary to the principles of analogy through recognition of more persuasive rationales based on the *Qur'an*, *sunna* and *ijtihad* or interpretation, while taking into account public interest.¹⁷

The *Qur'an* states that "Those who listen to the Word, and then follow the best it contains, are the ones who have been guided by God" (Q.XXXIX:18).

---

8. 'Abd al-Hamid, *supra* note 6, at 128; *see also*, 'Abd al-Wahhab Khallaf, *Masadir al-Tashri' al-Islami fima la Nassa fihi* (Kuwait 1970), p. 19.
9. *See, e.g.*, Joseph Schacht, *Introduction to Islamic Law* (London 1964), pp. 37, 60.
10. *See* Joseph Schacht, *The Origins of Muhammedan Jurisprudence* (Oxford 1975), p. 98; *see also* N.J. Coulson, *A History of Islamic Law* (Edinburgh 1964), p. 40; Subhi Mahmassani, *The Philosophy of Jurisprudence in Islam*, tr. Farhat J. Ziadeh (Leiden 1961), p. 85.
11. *See* Ahmad Hasan, *The Early Development of Islamic Jurisprudence* (Islamabad 1970), p. 145.
12. *See* Mohammad Hashim Kamali, *Principles of Islamic Jurisprudence* (Cambridge 1991), pp. 245, 404.
13. 'Abd al-'Aziz al-Bukhari, *Kashf al-Asrar* (Istanbul 1307), Vol. 3, p. 1123.
14. al-Sarakhsi, *al-Mabsut* (Beirut 1978), Vol. 10, p. 145.
15. al-Sarakhsi, *al-Usul* (Beirut 1973), Vol. 2, p. 200.
16. *See, e.g.*, Ibn Taymiya, *al-Musawwada fi Usul al-Fiqh* (Cairo 1983), pp. 401-404; al-Shatibi, *al-I'tisam* (Cairo 1932), Vol. 2, pp. 138-140; Khallaf, *supra* note 7, at 69-72.
17. Ibrahim Kafi Dönmez, *Islam Hukukunda Muctehidin Naslar Karsisindaki Durumuile Modern Hukuklarda Hakimin Kanun Karsisindaki Durumu Aras nda Bir Mukayese,* in Marmara Üniversitesi Ilahiyat Fakültesi Dergisi (Istanbul 1986), Vol. 4, p. 42; Abdulkadir Sener, *Kiyas Istihsan Istislah* (Ankara 1974), p. 67; Kamali, *supra* note 11, at 245-247.

For example, although the Prophet prohibited the sale of goods not physically available at the time of the transaction,[18] he permitted the commercial practices of "*salam*"[19.] These practices are transactions whose subject is future goods. The sale of future goods represents an important tool for commercial predictability while guarding against fraud, the utility of which has long been recognized. Consequently, Islam developed this mechanism to permit those types of contracts while maintaining the core principles underlying the general prohibitions.[20]

Similarly, the *Caliph* 'Umar opened an irrigation canal by force, flooding the field of a property owner who denied its use to his neighbor.[21] This case illustrates the power of the sovereign to set aside normative judgment in order to resolve a situation on the basis of justice and equity, balancing the private property interests with the magnitude of potential loss to be incurred by the neighbor.

Some schools of Islamic law, in particular the *Hanafis*, have placed great reliance on the doctrine of *istihsan* where strict adherence to the letter of the law would lead to unjust consequences. They considered the position of *istihsan* within the broader framework of general principles of Islamic law and the consensus of Muslims, in order to achieve justice. Thus, Abu Hanifa (d.150/767), considered the issue of witnesses testifying regarding alleged acts of fornication. If the witnesses' perspective is from different vantage points, the strict viewpoint held that the crime of fornication was not established, and that the witnesses were themselves subject to punishment for false accusations of unchastity. However, Abu Hanifa felt that since such a judgment would be contrary to the principle of punishing the criminals, and contrary to basic conceptions of justice, the testimony of these four witnesses should be accepted through *istihsan*, and the criminals punished for fornication.[22]

One of the established principles of Islamic law is that a trusted person cannot be held responsible for payment of damages, in the same manner as the person with whom a good was deposited is not held responsible. Because goods held by a partner, or leased by a tenant, as well as equipment used by workers and artists are considered to be deposited with them, such parties are not held responsible for the loss of goods, in the absence of negligence or intentional casualty.[23] However Abu Yusuf (d.182/198) and Shaybani held that artists and

---

18. Al-Bukhari, *al-Jami 'al-Sahih*, ed. Krehl (Leiden) 1864, vol. 2, pp. 4 f.f.

19. *Salam* is a future sale of goods in which the price is fixed in advance but the delivery is postponed.

20. al-Sarakhsi, *al-Usul*, *supra* note 14, at 203.

21. Malik, *supra* note 3, at 122.

22. al-Shatibi *supra* note 15, at 140-141.

23. Mustafa Ahmad al-Zarqa, *al-Fiqh al-Islami fi Thawbihi al-Jadid* (Damascus 1967), Vol. 1, p. 54.

artisans must compensate the owner for the loss of such goods, even in the absence of fault, but would not be held responsible for casualty due to natural disasters. These two distinguished jurists, despite the principle that a "deposited good is not compensated," held through *istihsan* that compensation must be paid in order to protect the property and to prevent fraud and exploitation.[24] Other issues which have been considered in light of *istihsan* include whether the excrement of wild birds may be found to be clean, the legality of receiving the payment for religious services, the donation of transferable properties, and the right of compensation for the property seized from orphans, trusts and estates. Factors evaluated in the application of *ishtihan* in these examples include such moral points as the needs of people, public interest, necessity, equity and justice. Both the *Maliki* and *Hanafi* jurists accepted *istihsan*, and even the *Shafi'i* jurists, who opposed *istihsan* etymologically, utilized similar methodology under the name of *qiyas* or *istishab* to achieve similar outcome-driven conclusions.

Even through the widely employed practice of dividing *istihsan* into three components, (1) according to *sunna*, (2) custom and consensus, and (3) necessity; and, considering these components outside of *istihsan al-qiyas*, one is not fully able to explain the judicial foundation upon which *istihsan* is based. *Istihsan* is, in fact, a practice of harmonizing specific judgments with the general principles of the *Qur'an* and *sunna* – a reconsideration of the judgments emphasizing considerations of equity and justice reflecting the human spirit. In a close reading, the form of judgment which was primarily referred to as "clear analogy" was not really taken seriously, but only that it consists of the implementation of one of the rules as a secondary incident. But, when the rule is applied by considering only judicial merits, without taking into consideration factual equity, consequent results, and the conformity of the outcome with equity and justice, the desired result cannot be attained. Therefore, the outcome is moderated by the application of equity and justice in interpreting religious texts and establishing new judgments.

Here, the dualism of "reality-ideal" which was not mentioned as far as written sources of Islamic law are concerned, emerges as positive law (just law). This, to a degree, is a stage of considering the principle of equity, after dispensing justice which is inherent in the concept of "justice" as a first principle of natural law. In other words, this represents an effort to furnish the principles of rational law, as it developed in Europe in the 19th and the 20th centuries, with a social dimension.

The high priority that the *Hanafi* jurists have placed on reason in the issue of *husn* and *qubh* has greatly affected their frequent application of *istihsan*. For example, al-Ghazzali (d.505/1111), a *Shafi'i* jurist, criticized Abu Hanifa

---

24. al-Kasani, *Bad'ayi'* (Beirut 1974), Vol. 4, p. 120.

for his acceptance of the testimony of four witnesses to fornication who nevertheless had different perspectives, but stated that Abu Hanifa had based his argument merely on the principle of the "ugliness of proving false [testimony] of Muslims..."[25] It is remarkable that Ibn Rushd (d.595/1198) considered *istihsan* as "returning to justice and public interest."[26]

ISTISLAH (PUBLIC INTEREST)

The term "*istislah*" is derived from the Arabic root-letters "*s-l-h*", which literally means "wishing the improvement, amendment and correction of something." In Islamic jurisprudence, it refers to the practice of arriving at a decision based on perceived public interest, where there is neither legislative guidance as to that particular interest, nor is there controlling religious text or consensus. In essence, *istislah* is judgment based on public interest.[27]

The laws of Islam are rooted in compelling social reason and aim at the achievement of a basic, collective good and the welfare of human beings. Unfortunately, legislators are not consistent in providing the rationales for their laws. Where they are silent, this rationale must be ascertained through human comprehension and perception. Muslim jurists have tried to apply revealed reason in similar cases. Whenever certain judgments lack revealed reason, the jurists first sought to establish the reason underlying the judgment and then to ascertain the breadth of applicability. All of these efforts have been made under the name of *analogy*. In contrast, *istislah* is employed where there is neither a judgment by the *shari'* (legislator), nor an established rationale and public policy to be utilized for the given factual situation. In other words, it is up to human discretion to establish a judgment and state the rationale upon which judgment is based, and the societal goal that the judgment effectuates. In fact, the reason why it is called "*al-maslaha al-mursala*" is because the interest it is based upon is not subject to any condition or restriction.[28]

The Islamic religion sought to protect five basic principles, "religion", "life", "reason", "generation," and "property", in order to maintain social order and provide a peaceful and secure life for the people. In fact, almost all religions and systems of positive law are in agreement on the necessity of the protection and promotion of these five principles. In Islamic law, these principles are referred to as the "indispensable interests" or "fundamental pur-

---

25. al-Ghazali, *al-Mustasfa* (Bulaq 1324), Vol. 1, pp. 281-282.
26. al-Zarqa, *supra* note 23, at 88.
27. Khallaf, *supra* note 7, at 88. *See also*, Mahmassani, *supra* note 9, at 87, al-Zarqa, *supra* note 23, at 1,90.
28. 'Abd al-Hamid, *supra* note 6, at 175-176. *See also* Khallaf, *supra* note 7, at 88.

poses of the *Shari'a*."²⁹ Religious laws and practices, permissions and prohibitions, and religious sanctions are all designed to protect and promote these principles. Secondarily, there are additional interests, which are intended to solve problems and satisfy the needs of human beings, and to facilitate the realization of the aims of the five principles. These are referred to as "complementary" interests (*hajiyat*). In addition, there are certain interests, referred to as "embellishments" (*tahsiniyat*),³⁰ which deal with the moral accomplishments of human beings and their virtues and manners. Consequently, judgments based on *istislah* take these interests into account and seek to arrive at a just decision which effectuates these societal interests while remaining acceptable under Islamic law. The basic aim of *istislah* is to effectuate these interests while preventing corruption, which is the antithesis of the five indispensable interests.

In a sense, all judgments are based on some considerations of public interests and equity. However, the concepts of group interest and harm which are taken into account when arriving at a judgment, are subject to changes of time and society. It is necessary to accommodate the intention of the legislator in the light of changing circumstances and situations, while reexamining the concepts of public interest and corruption. For example, the *Caliph* Abu Bakr collected scattered pages of the *Qur'an* and fought against those refusing to pay *zakat*. The *Caliph* 'Umar did not distribute the occupied lands of Iraq among soldiers but instead returned them to the previous owners in return for the payment of taxes for the treasury. He did not distribute shares to the "*muallafat al-qulub*,"³¹ ordered the execution of every individual member of a group who killed someone intentionally, and chose not to prosecute theft during the years of famine. Although the Prophet expressed the wish that wandering camels whose owners were unknown should be left alone, the *Caliph* 'Uthman sold these camels on behalf of the State and paid the owners who asserted claims, while the *Caliph* 'Ali collected these camels in a big stable, in order to protect them.³²

In the period following the first caliphs, Muslim jurists and founders of the schools of law examined judicial decisions and arrived at new processes based on public interest, welfare, and the prevention of evil.

Istislah, particularly as used by the *Maliki* school, found a wide range of uses, and it has gained a multi-functional content and processes for protecting

---

29. al-Shatibi, *al-Muwafaqat fi Usul al-Shari'a* (Beirut 1975), Vol. 2, p. 10. *See also* Kamali, *supra* note 11, at 271-275.

30. al-Shatibi, *supra* note 29 at 10-11; *see also* Kamali, *supra* note 11, at 272.

31. The term *"muallafat al-qulub"* refers to people who have been recently reconciled to Islam.

32. Abu al-Walid al-Baji, *al-Muntaqa* (Cairo 1331), Vol. 6, pp. 143-144. *See also*, Said Ramadan al-Buti, *Dawabit al-Maslaha* (Beirut 1982), p. 353.

public interest and preventing harm and evil in order to promote public welfare.³³

When considered from a natural law point of view, it may be observed that Muslim jurists, while using *istislah* and *maslaha*, have based their opinions on the basis of equity and justice, which are inherent in the human spirit and which finds expression in the general principles of Islam. *Istislah* and *istihsan* are theoretical concepts, compared with the process of judgment by consensus which is based on *de facto* agreement of Muslims and has rather an executive nature and custom (*'urf*). Judgments on the textual sources of Islamic law are motivated with certain aims and in accordance with public interest.³⁴ Religion itself is concerned with human beings and their interest. The scholar Najm al-Din al-Tufi (d.716/1316) argued that it is incumbent upon Allah to take the interest of human beings into account in his judgments and held that punishments should be based on religious texts and consensus while transactions should be based on interest. In other words, he considered human interest to be a stronger basis for decisions than not only consensus, but also textual sources.³⁵ By treating interest as a stronger proof than the *Qur'an* and *sunna*, he considered societal interest to be the real aim of law, while the religious texts are the means to this end.³⁶

CONCLUSION

The history of the Western philosophy of law arguably consists of little else other than the concepts of justice and natural law. Its jurisprudence has played an active role in shaping Western social and political thought and has formed the basis for criticism of positive law and its inevitable obsolescence. It is possible to explain this natural law and justice jurisprudence, which has been prevalent in Western thought, as a search for ideal law. However, it may be asserted that the search for ideal law may itself be an inherent aspect of human nature.

As for Islam, as indicated above, its jurisprudence contains the thought of a "most just and ideal law" as a derivation of the concepts of "absolute justice and *husn*," and the relationship between "positive and rational law-just law."

The most just and ideal law for a Muslim is divine equity and justice. Divine equity and justice, which are the components of absolute justice, will

---

33. Kamali, *supra* note 11, at 280. *See also* Schacht, *supra* note 8, at 61.
34. Ibn 'Abd al-Salam, *al-Qaw''id*, Vol. 1 p.9. *See also*, Khallaf, *supra* note 7, at 86-90; Mahmassani, *supra* note 9, at 106-107; Döonmez, *supra* note 16, at 42-43
35. al-Tufi, *Risala fi Ri'aya al-Maslaha*, (in Khallaf's *Masadir*), pp. 105-114.
36. *Id* at 141. *See also* al-Buti, *supra* note 32, at 205-215; al-Kamali, at 275-276.

fully and finally be implemented in the hereafter. Islam recognizes that absolute justice will not be realized in this world. Both the general principles of the *Qur'an* and its judgments, as related to private law, represent concrete forms of divine justice in relation to humans and their society, and these elements form the basis of positive law. Human beings, in spite of all unfavourable circumstances and effects, achieve the most just and ordered society, by basing it on these principles. Nevertheless, human effort alone will not achieve the most just and final law, but the process toward that end adds vitality to the development of positive law.

There are significant differences between intellectual concepts of equity and justice and the actual expressions of equity and justice in the social environment. This reflects, in a sense, the duality of the mind and body. Because the human mind comprehends conceptions of justice and equity through the filter of experience and analogy, pure justice remains an abstract and variable theory. However, *a priori*, divine equity and justice is absolute and free from subjective distortion. Thus, we discern an identification of the ideal law with divine justice and a partial identification of the jurisprudence of natural law with the divine sources of Islamic law. This partial identification, however, does not mean a total disappearance of the dualism of "reality-ideal," and of natural law, in Islamic law. Arguably, reason will advance this "ideal" from *Shar'ia* judgments, and by implementing this ideal in a variety of contexts and changing circumstances, the "reality" will come to resemble the "ideal". The legislator who attempts to support the human condition by seeking reason in the struggle for the "ideal" in *Shar'ia* judgments is guided by divine grace and compassion according to Muslim philosophers.

The example of natural law which appears to function as positive law criterion, means eventually to give way to many factors which exist in the formation of positive law, leading to the creation of serious gaps in the law. In other words, the development in the scope of natural law means an admission of the role of the human factor, which is a vicious circle according to the ontological philosophy of natural law. It seems inevitable that the principles of natural law should guide positive law and serve as its point of departure. These gaps serve to justify arbitrary decisions. This phenomenon has been frequently observed in the last few centuries, during which natural law was separated from divine law, and has become secular in nature, derived from human reason. For example, in the Middle Ages, usury was regarded as contrary to religious-natural law, and the people engaged in this business were criticized by the Church. Thus, it could be argued that Islam, through revelation, gave the idea of law a certain content, minimum principles and a starting point. This content, however, was legislated because it was indispensable, and the broad dualism of the "reality-ideal" is left for the implementation of a minimum number of principles. The explanation of the universality and liveliness of Islam is implied in this content. Both are based on criteria and analogy as strong as the criterion and bases are themselves strong.[37] For this reason, we defined the role of human reason by Islam on the basis of revelation as grace and divine assistance. Otherwise, it would be impossible to comprehend the role of such basic concepts as justice, freedom and equity, in the absence of a minimum criterion.

Over three hundred verses in the *Qur'an* contain the word "equity", as well as words derived from this root, and it has been frequently mentioned that Allah revealed the *Qur'an* through the Prophet by equity, Allah judges by equity, and has recommended the observance of equity to human beings. Likewise, "justice" and words derived from its root, are used in about thirty verses. As noted earlier, the understanding and implementation of these and similar general concepts of law depend on the capacity of human reason. The fact that the application of concepts of Islam displays different manifestations in different societies and remains valid for every society and age may well be explained in this context. Thus, Islamic law provided a wide field for the role of reason and philosophy of law.

In Islamic jurisprudence, the terminology of the *Qur'an* and *sunna* are closely scrutinized, under the title of terminological matters as well as by considering the rules of grammar. Efforts were made to understand and interpret these sources by considering such perspectives as sign, notion, indication, hint, content, as well as terminology. All of the factors are the result of the nature of the exercise of human intellect. Thus, we witness that rational results have been obtained by general rules, or by analogy, as well as by *"istihsan"* and *"istislah"*. Consequently, Muslims have tried to conceive the idea of equity and justice, hidden in the spirit of human being, with the help of all of these methodological processes. Moreover, the usage of *hiyal* in Islamic legal doctrine, also aims at realizing equity and justice, where a seemingly lawful act in accordance with the literal (external) meaning of the law, must nevertheless be in conformity with the spirit, or general purposes of the law.

Finally, we should bear in mind that the discussions on the concepts of *husn-qubh*, goodness-badness, or justice-tyranny, which are, in a sense, a discussion on "reality-ideal", have remained in the field of *kalam*. That this scholarly debate had almost disappeared in positive and especially in public law, and that rulers have gradually gained titles such as *"caliph"* or *"dhill Allah"* (the shadow of God), and therefore have obtained, to a degree, untouchability and indisputablity, may well be explained by the gradual integration of divine and human nature of Islamic law, and by conviction that the most just positive law has been obtained. Not only the great Muslim jurists, but also theological and political thinkers have contributed to the growth of a legal heritage as rich and impressive as Roman law.

---

37. *See* Khadduri, *supra* note 1, at 151-155.

Islamic Criminal Law

Muhammad Abu-Hassan[1]

INTRODUCTION

Islam seeks to establish a world community, with complete equality among peoples, without distinction of race, class, or country. The first thing which strikes the imagination is that Islamic law seeks to regulate the entire field of human life in its material as well as spiritual aspects. The law deals first with religious rites and practices and then with the rules governing the State and the Caliphate. It also deals with the relationship between believers and unbelievers within the Islamic State and the relationship between the Islamic State and other states. In dealing with the rights and duties of believers, Islamic law also provides rules for criminal actions. This essay deals specifically with the criminal law.

Islamic law divides human activities into five categories:

1. *Fard* or *Wajib* (Duty or Obligatory) – performance of these actions is rewarded, and its omission is punished.

2. *Mandub* (Recommended) – actions the performance of which is rewarded but the omission of which is not punished.

3. *Mubah* (Optional) – actions permitted by silence

4. *Makruh* (Disliked) – actions disapproved of but not punished.

5. *Haram* (Forbidden) – actions punishable by law.

EQUALITY UNDER ISLAMIC LAW

Equality under the law is an aspect of the general principle of equality. Law applies equally to everyone, without discrimination between individuals on the basis of sex, colour and wealth, kinship or friendship – even on the basis of creed, or anything else on which people differ. It has been expressed in a

---

1. Judge Muhammad Abu-Hassan of Amman, Jordan is a specialist in law and anthropology.

tradition from the Prophet. He said, "Destroyed were those among you who, when a high born among you committed a theft, pardoned him and when someone poor among them did it, imposed punishment on him. By God, even if Fatima, the daughter of Muhammad, were to steal, I would cut her hands."

All persons in the Islamic State are equal in the court of justice in terms of their submission to its rules. There is no discrimination between individuals in the legal process followed in establishing a claim, the principles of legal defense, the rules of evidence, application of rulings, implementation of orders, or the necessity for the investigation of the court between contesting parties. Even unbelievers, if they seek justice in Islamic courts, would be treated equally under the law. "[W]hen you judge among the people, do so equitably"(Q.IV:58).

Equality in the courts of justice was recognized to such an extent that a letter of 'Umar Ibn al-Khattab addressed to Abu Musa Al-Ash'ari reads: "Comfort people with your presence and through your contact, and in imparting justice so that no noble person is keen to insult you, and no weak person is dismayed by your justice." In a modern code, the Ottoman Civil Code, (the *Majalla)* states concerning the qualifications and conduct of judges:

> **Article 1792:** The judge must be intelligent, upright, reliable and firm.
>
> **Article 1793**: The judge must have a knowledge of Muhammadan law and jurisprudence and of the rules of procedure and must be able to decide and settle actions in accordance therewith.
>
> **Article 1794**: The judge must be of a perfect understanding. Consequently, any judicial act performed by a minor or an imbecile or a blind man or a person so deaf that he cannot hear the statements of the parties when speaking loudly, is invalid.
>
> **Article 1795**: The judge must abstain from any act or deed of a nature injurious to the dignity of the Court, such as engaging in buying or selling or making jokes while in Court.
>
> **Article 1796**: The judge may not accept a present from either of the parties.
>
> **Article 1797**: The judge may not accept the hospitality of either of the parties.
>
> **Article 1798**: The judge must abstain from any act during the trial likely to arouse suspicion or cause misunderstanding, such as receiving one of the parties alone in his house, or retiring with one of them to consider the judgment, or making signs to one of them with his hand or his eye or his head, or speaking to one of them secretly or in a language not understood by the other.
>
> **Article 1799**: The judge must be impartial towards the two parties. Consequently, the judge must observe complete impartiality and equality towards the two parties in everything relating to the trial of

the action, such as causing them to sit down during the course of the trial, and when looking towards or addressing them and this whether one of the parties is a person of high rank and the other of low estate.

THE ISLAMIC CONCEPT OF CRIME

According to Islamic jurisprudence, crime is defined as the violation of primary public and private rights. Crimes fall into two distinct categories, offenses against God, and offenses against private individuals. Offenses against God correspond to offenses against the public. There are only two divisions of rights under Islamic law, the rights of God and the rights of men. The obvious distinction between these rights is that the enforcement of the right of God is the duty of the State, while it is at the option of the individual whose private right has been infringed, to seek its enforcement or pardon the wrongdoer.

Under Islamic law, criminal offenses mostly concern issues relating to: (1) the person, (2) property, (3) honour, (4) the State, (5) religion, (6) public peace and tranquility, and (7) decency and morals. Before deciding whether or not a criminal should be punished, one must consider the extent of his responsibility for the offense he committed. Islamic law also takes into consideration the viewpoint of the person who committed the crime and that of the community against which the crime took place.

CRIME AND PUNISHMENT IN ISLAMIC LAW

Muslim jurists deal with punishment under three categories, (a) *hadd*, (b) *qisas*, and (c) *ta'zir*.

Hadd (Specific Penalties)

Hadd is defined in the *Hidaya*[2] as specific penalties for violation of the

---

2. *Hidaya* is a commentary upon *Bidayat-Al Mubtadi*, and both the text and the commentary were composed by Shaykh Burhan al-Din 'Ali, son of Abu Bakr of Murghinan, who took 13 years in the preparation of the latter work and died at the age of 62 in 593 Hijra (1197 A.D.). The importance of the *Hidaya* lies in its classification of the principles and arguments which have decided cases.

Hidaya was the Indian criminal law before the British Raj. It was the authoritative text not only in India but also in several other Muslim countries and was translated into English by Charles Hamilton and published in 1791.

It is important to note that *Hidaya* was one of the main sources of the Ottoman *Majalla* (the civil code of the Ottoman empire), which continued to be the civil law in Jordan until it was replaced by the new Jordanian civil law no. 43 in 1976, based on Islamic jurisprudence.

rights of God, or public rights. It is distinguished from *qisas*, the penalty for violation of the rights of man, or private justice. Under *hadd*, the quantity and quality of punishment is fixed for certain offenses – when it is determined by the *Qadi*[3] that the rights of God have been violated.

The aim of *hadd* is to deter people from the commission of acts which are injurious to the community. As this is a public right, the ruler or his deputy are exclusively authorized to enforce it, the claim and prosecution of the party injured is not indispensable, nor could the party remit, or discharge the prescribed penalty as in the case of *qisas*. But the execution of *hadd* is prevented when there is any doubt (*shubha*) or legal defect. In such a case, the *qadi* is directed to administer the law with moderation. *Hadd* punishment is applicable to the following crimes:

Zina (adultery) It is defined as "an unlawful conjunction of the sexes" and the punishment prescribed for the offense of zina, when legally established against a sane married man of sound understanding and mature in age, is lapidation or stoning to death; but if unmarried, the adulterer is subject to the sentence of one hundred lashes. The penalties for a man or woman in similar circumstances are to be applied in such a manner that the lashes strike different parts of the body, to avoid endangering the life of the recipient. Banishment or imprisonment for a limited period, in addition to flogging, was left to the discretion of the qadi.

It is nearly impossible to prove a charge of *zina*, because conviction for this crime requires the evidence of four honorable witnesses who actually saw the accused commit the proscribed act. In addition, after conviction, if the witnesses or any one of them declined to throw the first stone, the sentence could not be executed. Moreover, if a convict fled after receiving part of this punishment and was seized after a subsequent interval, the remaining punishment could not be enforced. *Hadd* for *zina,* therefore, was prevented by a lapse of time. Similarly, if a man had been guilty of several acts of *zina* and was punished for one, he could not be punished for the others.

Finally, in the case of doubt *(shubha)*, the sentence of *hadd* is barred. *Shubha* is defined as "that which appears to be just and right but in truth is not." *Shubha* in the context of *zina* falls into three broad categories:

(1) misconception of the act as legal when it was in fact illegal,
(2) *shubha* as a consequence to the actual existence of some ground of legality,
(3) a presumption of the validity of marriage.[4]

---

3. A *qadi* is an Islamic judge. *See* David A. Westbrook, *Islamic International Law and Public International Law: Separate Expressions of World Order*, 33 VA. J. INT'L L. 819, 896 (1993).

4. According to Abu-Hanifa, this was sufficient to exempt the parties from the punishment of *hadd*, whether the parties knew the marriage to be legal or not. But his disciples maintained that if the parties married with full knowledge of the illegality of the contract, they should therefore be subject to *hadd* penalties.

The *hadd* punishment by stoning in cases of adultery was not specified in the text of the *Qur'an*, and therefore the *Khawarij* jurists and some of the *Shi'ite* and *Mu'tazila* jurists reject it as punishment for adultery. In addition, several modern authorities of Islamic jurisprudence including al-Alusi, Muhammad Abu-Zahra, and Mustafa al-Zarqa reject this doctrine on the basis of *shubha* or doubt as to its legality.[5]

Qadhf (accusation of adultery) The term "*qadhf*" means "accusation", which in the legal context means to levy a charge of adultery against a married man or woman. The person so acting is called the *qadhif* or slanderer, and the man or woman so accused is called the *maqdhuf/maqdhufa* or slandered.

Accusing a lady of fornication not only damages her reputation, but also creates bad blood between families, renders parentage doubtful, spoils conjugal relations and is harmful to the peace of mind. Consequently, the *qadhif* is required to produce four witnesses in support of his accusation. If he fails to prove his charge, he receives eighty lashes and is prevented from ever again appearing as a witness. Some conditions are required for punishment of the *qadhif*. First, the slandered man or woman should be sane and of sound judgment. Second, the slandered man or woman should be of a mature age because both minors and those who are mentally deficient may not be accused of adultery as it cannot be proven in their case.

Because both private and public rights are implicated in cases of slander, it is mandatory for the slandered individual to pursue the charge and demand that the false accuser be punished. In addition, the claimant must attend the execution of the sentence in person. *Hadd* for slander is not prevented by a lapse of time and cannot be imposed without the claim of the party aggrieved.

Sariqa (theft) *Sariqa* is defined as larceny by stealth. According to the *Hidaya*, the crime of *sariqa* was defined as a responsible, sane adult person who wrongfully and furtively takes the undisputed property of another, when such property is in due custody, and the value of it is not less than ten *dirhams*. To constitute theft the following elements are essential:

First, the thief must be a sane adult. The *Hadd* punishment of amputation of the thief's hand cannot be enforced against an infant or person of unsound mind.

Second, the type of custody required to prove theft must be either (a) "custody of place" – the theft must be from a place which was generally used for the custody of the property stolen; or (b) "personal guard" – the taking must be from the control of a person of property.

Finally, the property must be of some value which must be not less than the prescribed *nisab* (limit).

---

5. *See* 'Ali 'Ali Mansur, *Al-Tajrim wa al-'Iqab fi al-Islam* 179 (1976). Judge 'Ali Mansur was formerly the President of the Egyptian Constitutional Court. *See also*, Faqih 'Abdul-Rahman Al Jaziri, *Al-Fiqh 'Ala al Madhahib al Arba'a*, Vol. V, pp. 8-9.

The penalty imposed for the first offense of *sariqa* is the amputation of right hand of the thief at the wrist, and for the second offense, amputation of the left foot. If the thief continues to commit *sariqa*, he is imprisoned for life or until he shows signs of rehabilitation.

However, the application of *hadd* was subject to a number of restrictions. For example, a person stealing the property of his or her parents, or any of their ancestors or descendants was not subject to amputation. Similarly, the punishment was not administered for the theft of property of any direct relation, unless it was taken from the house of a stranger. Conversely, amputation was not administered for stealing the property of a stranger from the house of a direct relation.

A husband or wife stealing each other's property were not subject to amputation. Nor was it administered for the theft of property from a public bath or public house, because of the lack of custody; however, it was administered for theft from these places at night when strangers were not allowed access. If a guest stole the property of his host, he was not subject to amputation, as he was allowed to enter the house, and his offense was considered to be treachery rather than theft.

A breach of trust did not give rise to the penalty of amputation, nor was it incurred by openly seizing or snatching away a thing, for such an act was not considered to be theft. Furthermore, if a person stole property of which he was a part-owner, he was not liable to amputation. And on the same principle, the penalty was not invoked for theft from the public treasury, as it was considered to be common property of the Muslims, each of whom had a share in it.

A sentence of amputation could not be passed upon a thief without the attendance and prosecution of the person whose property had been stolen or his representative. If the stolen property was returned by a thief to the owner before any prosecution was instituted against him, he could not be sentenced to suffer amputation. Amputation was also estopped if, after sentencing, the market value of the stolen property fell below the legal standard of *nisab* (ten *dirhams*). One punishment for theft by amputation, as in all other cases of *hadd*, included all past instances. However, it did not preclude further punishment for any future repetition of the offense.

Sariqa Kubra (*highway robbery*) Four classes of highway robbers were specified in the *Hidaya*. First, those who were seized before they had robbed, murdered, or frightened anyone were to be imprisoned by the *qadi* until they demonstrated evident signs of repentance. Second, those who committed robbery only and not murder were to have their right hand and left foot amputated, provided the property taken amounted to ten *dirhams* per each robber.

For those who committed murder without robbery, forgiveness of the legal heir of the slain was immaterial, because of the social deterrent effect of punishment. Finally, for those who committed both robbery and murder, it was optional to the *qadi* either to cut off a hand and foot and then put them to death or to put them to death at once without amputation. If any member of a gang of robbers committed murder, the whole group was subject to the prescribed penalty.

Shurb al-Khamr This literally means the drinking of wine. Under Islamic law, drinking any quantity, however small, is a criminal act. In the case of other forms of liquor, it is necessary to drink a quantity sufficient to become intoxicated. A difference of opinion existed between Abu Hanifa and his two disciples, Abu Yusuf and Shaybani, as to the degree of intoxication which is punishable. Abu Hanifa maintained that the party must be so intoxicated as not to understand what was said to him or to be unable to distinguish a man from a woman, while the latter considered penal drunkenness to be sufficiently established by confused and incoherent speech, the usual sign of intoxication.

The punishment for drinking wine or being intoxicated with other prohibited liquors is eighty lashes, to be administered in the same manner as in cases of *zina*. Only sane adults who are capable of speech may be held liable for the stated penalty, which is not to be inflicted during intoxication. Non-Muslims are not punished by *hadd* for drinking wine, since it is not prohibited by their religion. There are different *fiqh* opinions among the different Muslim sects concerning the crime of *shurb al-khamr*.[6]

Al-Ridda (apostasy) Apostasy in Islamic law means turning from Islam after being a Muslim. It occurs either through words or deeds which put an end to one's adherence to Islam, such as the rejection of fundamental principles of faith, the existence of Allah or the prophecy of Muhammad as contained in the formula of the profession of the faith: "There is no God but Allah and Muhammad is His Apostle."

It is very important to know that apostasy has two faces: one is religious, i.e., against Islam as religion, and the other face is political, i.e., against the Islamic state as a state. Here, we limit dealing with apostasy as a political criminal case which violates the constitution of the state and as such it has no relation with the freedom of belief or religion.

According to Islamic law, a male apostate is to be put to death while a female apostate is not subject to capital punishment, but may be kept in prison until she repents. There is a consensus of opinion among Muslim jurists that clear evidence is required of apostasy. The apostate is not immediately put to death, but is given a fair chance to explain his viewpoint and every effort is made to convince him of his wrong act and bring him to repentance. The jurists also hold that no one is to be treated as an apostate unless he is of mature age and is not subject to any pressure. The punishment for apostasy, by definition, is applicable only to Muslims.

---

6. Muhammad Abu Hassan, *Crime and Punishment in Islamic Jurisprudence* (Amman 1987), pp. 295-330.

Qisas (retaliation)

Retaliation was prevalent in pre-Islamic Arabia, based on the assumption that retaliation is a vindication of public and private rights. Retaliation represents infliction of a similar injury to the wrongdoer by the injured person or their heirs. It is equivalent to the maxim of the Mosaic law, an eye for an eye and a tooth for a tooth.[7] As retaliation is viewed as a individual right of the private person or his heirs, the law allows that the offender may be discharged on payment of compensation and may also be pardoned. In certain cases the offender's tribe, *the aqila,* is called upon to pay blood money to the heirs of the deceased. Retaliation is also authorized for wounding, rather than killing another, as the *Qur'an* states: "[A]nd for wounds, retribution..." (Q.V:45).

Homicide

Islamic law recognizes five distinct types of homicide:

Qatl Al-'Amd (wilful murder). Islamic law presumes that any sane person who intentionally kills a person with a weapon[8], is a sinner deserving perdition according to the Qur'an and that the murderer is subject to retaliation.

The Arabic term "*qisas*" stands for the forfeiture of life for a life in the case of murder; however, it does not mean that the murderer should be killed in the manner in which he committed the murder. It only means that his life should be taken as he took the life of the other. Once wilful homicide is proved, no distinction is made between passionate and premeditated murder.

According to Islamic law, murder is a dischargeable offense. Although retaliation is the prescribed punishment for wilful murder, the heirs or next of kin can either forgive or discharge the offense. If the decedent's heir was a minor or person of diminished mental capacity, then his or her father is entitled to demand retaliation. On the other hand, having once accepted a money payment in discharge of the murder, the relatives of the slain person are strictly forbidden from any future acts of revenge against the killer. In the case of wilful homicide, the murderer cannot inherit the property of the victim.

The purpose of *qisas* is the protection of the individual and society rather than revenge. Islam, through the practice of *qisas,* suppresses crime while permitting the exercise of benevolence and mercy.

Qatl Shibh al-'Amd (manslaughter). This is a form of wilful murder where the perpetrator strikes a man with something which is neither a weapon nor serves as one. It resembles wilful homicide in the voluntariness of the act but differs from it by the use of an instrument which is not considered to endanger

---

7. *See Exodus* 21:24.
8. Or some object serving as a weapon.

life, so that malevolent intent cannot be presumed. Manslaughter is held to be sinful and to require atonement. It also excludes the actor from inheriting the property of the deceased.

Qatl al-Khata' (*erroneous homicide*). The erroneous homicide and the error which distinguishes it from the two preceding classes might be error in the act or error in intention. Error in the act occurs when a person intends a particular act and another act occurs, such as when a person shoots an arrow at a target, and it hits a man. Error in intention is where the mistake occurs not in the act but with respect to the subject. For example, when a person shoots an arrow at a man believing him to be game is required to free a Muslim slave or fast for two consecutive months and to pay a fine within three years. He also cannot he inherit the property of the deceased.

Qatl Qa'im Maqam Khata' (*involuntary homicide*). This is a form of erroneous homicide, an example of which, given in the *Hidaya*, is of a sleeping person who falls on another and thereby kills him. Other examples include where a brick or a piece of wood accidentally falls from the hand of a person.

Qatl bi Sabab (*accidental homicide*). This form occurs when, for instance, a man digs a well which another falls into and dies. In this case, a fine must be paid but atonement is not required, and the actor may inherit from the deceased. Thus, in Islamic law wilful murder, unintentional manslaughter and personal injury, without exception, may be discharged by the payment of damages.

Ta'zir (prohibition)

The legal definition of *ta'zir* means punishment decreed by *Shar'ia* either on account of the right of God or of the individual. It is discretionary punishment ranging from fines and corporal punishment to imprisonment. *Ta'zir* gives a wide latitude to the *qadi* in imposing sentence, and the entire system of Islamic criminal law, *asasiat al-shari'a,* is based upon it.

The final principle of punishment is *ta'zir* and *siyasa,*[9] where the form and extent of punishment rest entirely at the discretion of the *qadi*. Under *ta'zir,* the punishment could range from imprisonment or banishment to public exposure. This punishment is designed primarily to deter a criminal from committing further crimes and secondarily to reform him.

Islamic criminal law vests in the sovereign the power to sentence criminals to *ta'zir* punishment in three circumstances. First, *ta'zir* punishment may be imposed in the case of offenses for which no specific penalty of *hadd* or *qisas* has been provided by the law. Second, *ta'zir* may be administered for

---

9. "Discretionary and exemplary" punishment.

crimes covered under *hadd* and *qisas*, when proof of the commission of such crimes may not be sufficient to impose specific penalties, although it is sufficient to establish a strong presumption of guilt. Similarly *ta'zir* is appropriate when the proof is sufficient to support a sentence of *hadd* or *qisas*, but when such sentence is barred by retaliation in cases of *qisas*, or by doubt (*shubha*), which bars judgment for the specific penalty in Islamic law. Thirdly, *ta'zir* is appropriate for punishment of heinous crimes which are injurious to society – particularly for repeated offenses of these crimes, which public justice may appear to require exemplary punishment beyond the prescribed penalties.

Ta'zir penalties fall into two categories, the satisfaction of private or individual rights, and public rights, considered to be rights of God. While private injuries may be excused by the injured party, only the sovereign may commute punishment of a criminal, provided the offender repents before punishment. Unlike *hadd* and *qisas* punishments, *ta'zir* punishments are not specific and can include *al-wa'dh* (admonition), *al-tawbikh* (reprimand), *al-tahdid* (threat), *al-hajr* (boycott), *al-tashir* (public disclosure), *al-gharama wal musadara* (fine and seizure of property), *al-habs* (imprisonment), *al-jald* (flogging), and even *al-ta'zir bil-qatl* (death penalty).

Diya (blood money)

Diya means a fine or compensation for blood in cases of homicide. The punishment of *qisas* in all cases of wilful homicide may be discharged by payment of *diya*, at the option of the decedent's heirs, with the end being relief and satisfaction of mind. All illegal homicides, with the exception of wilful homicide for which retaliation cannot be claimed, can be satisfied with *diya*, or the fine of blood payable by the offender or his *'aqila*.

In cases of quasi-deliberate homicide, erroneous homicide, or involuntary homicide, in addition to the payment of *diya*, the offender must atone for their offense and may not inherit from the deceased. However, in the case of accidental homicide, no other punishment is added to the payment of *diya* as culpability does not attach to any person.

Offenses against the person short of homicide, which do not give rise to the right of retaliation, subject the offender, if the act is involuntary, to the payment of *arsh* or *diya*. Both *qisas* and *arsh* for non-life threatening injuries were subject negotiation between the parties according to the same principles of private right and satisfaction applicable in cases of homicide.

A difference of religion, however, did not bar retaliation, as Muslims and non-Muslim subjects had an equal right of self-protection. And according to the *Hidaya*, there is no difference between the fine for death of a Muslim and that of a non-Muslim subject.

NOTES:

1. Before the advent of the British, the penal law prevailing in India was Islamic law, and yet up to 1862, when the Indian penal code came into operation, Islamic law was the basis of the criminal law.
2. Islamic Criminal Law continued to operate, in the Ottoman Empire until 1858, when it was replaced by the French penal code which was issued in 1810.
3. "Until the Eighteenth Century, the Islamic Criminal Law was superior to the English Criminal Law. Tapas Kumar Bonerjee, *Background to Indian Criminal Law* (Orient Longmans, New Delhi), p. 67.

BIBLIOGRAPHY

Muhammad Abu-Hassan, *Crime and Punishment in Islamic Jurisprudence*, (Amman 1987).
Tapas Kumar Bonerjee, *Background to Indian Criminal Law* (Orient Longmans, New Delhi).
Abdur Rahman I. Doi, *Shari'ah The Islamic Law* (Ta Ha Pub., London 1984).
Mohamed S. El-Awa, *Punishment in Islamic Law* (American Trust Pub. 1982).
Anwar Ahmad Qadri, *Islamic Jurisprudence in the Modern World (A Reflection Upon Comparative Study of the Law)* (N.M. Tripathi Private Booksellers & Pub., Bombay)
Mohammad Iqbal Siddiqi, *The Penal Law of Islam* (International Islamic Pub., New Delhi 1988).
Mohammad Al-Haj Ullah, *The Administration of Justice in Islam: An Introduction to the Muslim Conception of the State* (Nusrat Ali Nasri, New Delhi 1986).

Jihad as a Concept of Just War[1]

Majid Khadduri

To anyone who heard the leaders of "Hizb Allah", "Hamas", "Islamic Jihad" and other extremist groups calling Muslim believers to arms against their enemies, it will be exceedingly hard to believe that Islam's dreaded "holy war" is not the frightful summons to massacre that the Western nations have historically believed. Yet the truth is that the *jihad* – popularly called "holy war" – is largely a religious-legal duty aimed as much at spiritual salvation as the defence of the Islamic state.

It is ironic that the concept of "holy war" as a means to extend religious influence, which now alarms the West, was also a Western concept of holy war when Christendom had sent army after army storming the Holy Land (Palestine) and called them Crusaders. Yet the West persisted to recoil from the concept of *jihad* and has ever since, as Gibbon, in his *Decline and Fall of the Roman Empire*, colorfully but inaccurately wrote, "Muhammad, with the sword in one hand and the Koran in the other, erected his throne on the ruins of Christianity and Rome."[2] Like other wars, the *jihad*, whenever it was declared in a contest with other nations, an element of violence was certainly used. But the violence in the *jihad* is not the whole story, as it also has its own spiritual elements.

Strictly speaking, the word jihad does not mean "war" in the material sense of the word. Literally, it means "exertion", "effort" and "attempt", denoting that the believer is urged to use his utmost endeavors to fulfill a certain function or carry out a specific task. Its technical meaning is the exertion of the believer's strength to fulfill a duty prescribed by the law in "the path of God"

---

1. Most of the material in this paper has been freely drawn from my *War and Peace in the Law of Islam* (1955); *The Islamic Conception of Justice* (1984), Chap. 7; and an article on *"The Greater War"*, in *Aramco World Magazine*, July-August, 1968, pp. 24-27.

2. Edward Gibbon, *The History of the Decline and Fall of the Roman Empire*, ed. J.B. Bury (London, 1876), Vol. V, p. 435.

(Q.LXI:10-13)[3], the path of right and justice. The *jihad* may therefore be defined as a religious and legal duty which must be fulfilled by each believer either by the heart and tongue in combating evil and spreading the word of God, or by the hand and sword in the sense of participating in fighting. Only in the latter sense did Islam consider the *jihad* a collective duty (*fard al-kifaya*) which every believer was bound to fulfill, provided he was able to take the field. Believers who could not take the field nor had the means to do so were expected to contribute weapons or supplies in lieu of fighting with the sword. Participation in the *jihad* in one form or another was a highly-prized duty and the believer's recompence, if he actually took to the field, would be the achievement of salvation and reward of Paradise (Q.LXI:10-13) in addition to material rewards. Such war, called in Western legal tradition "just war" (*bellum justum*), is the only valid kind of war. All other wars are prohibited.

Even in the sense of fighting, *jihad* was not considered in the eyes of the Prophet Muhammad, as the primary duty of believers; fighting, in his eyes, was the lesser *jihad*. In a tradition from the Prophet, it states:

> Upon his return to Madina from a campaign, the Prophet Muhammad remarked: "We have just fulfilled the lesser *jihad*; it is now our duty to embark on the greater *jihad*."
> "What is the greater *jihad*?", asked one of his companions.
> "It is the struggle to save one's own soul," replied the Prophet.

The *jihad* in the sense of resort to violence was not introduced into the cradle of Islam by the Prophet Muhammad. It was already there as a tribal tradition of warfare – tribal raiding for economic motivation or revenge – for which Islam laid down rules for use by the state to achieve legitimate purposes in accordance with its own scale of justice. The Islamic state, composed of a community of believers endowed with a message to all men, was a universal state. Its public order, derived from and exercised on behalf of God, was potentially capable of governing the whole of mankind. The state thus was the instrument with which Islam sought to achieve its ultimate objective – the establishment of God's will and justice over the world.

But the Islamic universal state, not unlike other universal states, could not establish peace and order in the world solely with its scale of justice. Outside it, there remained other communities with which it had to deal permanently. The world was split into two divisions: the *dar al-Islam* (house of Islam), consisting of the territory over which Islamic justice ruled supreme, and the

---

3. Several translations of the *Qur'an* are available in the English language. Richard Bell, *The Qur'an* (Edinburgh, 1937-39), 2 Vols., is the nearest to the original Arabic structure; A.J. Arberry, *The Koran Interpreted* (London, 1955), 2 Vols., is a literary translation. Earlier translations by J.M. Rodwell (Everyman's Library) and E.H. Palmer (World's Classics) are useful.

rest of the world, called the *dar al-harb* (house of war), over which other public orders prevailed. The *dar al-harb* was the object, not the subject, of Islam, and it was the duty of the *Caliph*, head of the Islamic state, to extend the validity of its law and justice to the unbelievers by the *jihad*, not necessarily by resort to war, but, as noted earlier, by peaceful means.

The *dar al-Islam* was in theory neither at peace nor necessarily in permanent hostility with the *dar al-harb*, but in a condition which might be described as a "state of war", to use a modern legal terminology, because the ultimate objective of Islam was to establish peace and justice with the communities which acknowledged the Islamic public order. But the *dar al-harb*, though viewed as in a state of nature, was not treated as a no-man's land without regard to justice. Islam proposed to regulate its relationship with the *dar al-harb* in accordance with its law and justice.

The *jihad* was the just war (*bellum justum*) of Islam. God commanded the believers to spread His word and establish His law and justice over the world (Q.IX:5). But resort to war was subject to rules and limitations which believers were under obligations to observe in order that it would be a just war. Religion was and still is to be offered to other people by peaceful means, as there should be no compulsion of religion in the spread of the word of God (Q.II:256). The expansion of the state, carried out by the *jihad*, was a duty prescribed in the Islamic religion, and law was surely as pious and just as *pium* and *justum* in the way described by St. Augustine and St. Thomas, and later by Hugo Grotius.

In early Islam, jurists and other scholars like Abu Hanifa (d. 768), Malik (d. 795) and Shaybani (d. 804), made no explicit declarations that the *jihad* was a war to be waged against non-Muslims solely on the grounds of disbelief. On the contrary, they stressed that tolerance should be shown to unbelievers, especially the scripturaries (people who had a scripture, like Christians and Jews), and advised the *Caliph* to wage war when the inhabitants of the *dar al-harb* came into conflict with Islam. It was Shafi'i (d. 820) who formulated the doctrine that the *jihad* had for its intent the waging of war on unbelievers for their disbelief and not only because they entered into conflict with the Islamic state. The object of the *jihad*, which was not necessarily an offensive war, was thereby transformed into a collective obligation enjoined on the Islamic community to fight unbelievers "wherever you may find them" (Q.IX:5), and the distinction between offensive and defensive war became no longer relevant.

Shafi'i's doctrine, however, was not fully accepted by other scholars. For example, Tahawi (d. 933), disagreeing with Shafi'i, insisted that fighting was obligatory only when Muslims became involved with unbelievers[4]; while Sarakhsi, the great commentator on Shaybani's *Siyar* (based on Hanafi doctrines) accepted Shafi'i's doctrine of the *jihad* that fighting the unbelievers was

---

4. Al-Tahawi, *Kitab al-Mukhtasar*, ed. al-Afghani (Cairo, 1950), p. 281.

a "duty enjoined permanently until the end of time."⁵ Scholars who came afterwards, until the fall of Baghdad, then the capital of Islam, at the hands of the Mongols in 1258, accepted the *jihad* as just war without regard to its offensive or defensive character.

The Shaf'i doctrine of the *jihad* made no distinction between defensive and offensive war, for in the pursuance of the establishment of God's sovereignty and justice on Earth the distinction between defensive and offensive acts was irrelevant. However, although the duty of the *jihad* was commanded by God (Q.LXI:10-13), it was considered to be binding only when the strength of the believers was theirs (Q.II:233). When Islamic power began to decline, the state obviously could no longer assume a preponderant attitude without impairing its internal unity. Some scholars argued that the mere preparation for the *jihad* would be the fulfillment of the obligation. Not only did Islam become preoccupied with problems of internal security, but also its territorial integrity was exposed to dangers when foreign forces (Crusaders and Mongols) from the *dar al-harb* challenged its power and threatened its very existence.

In those altered circumstances, scholars began to review the meaning of the doctrine of the *jihad,* and the distinction between defensive and offensive war retained little of its substance. Ibn Taymiya (d. 1328), a jurist-theologian who was gravely concerned with internal disorder, understood the futility of the classical concept of *jihad* at a time when foreign enemies (Crusaders and Mongols) were menacing at the gates of *dar al-Islam*. He made a concession to reality by reinterpreting the *jihad* to mean waging a defensive war against unbelievers whenever they threatened Islam. Unbelievers who made no attempt to encroach upon the *dar al-Islam*, he asserted, were not the objective of Islam nor should the law and religion of Islam be imposed on them by force. "If the unbeliever were to be killed unless he becomes a Muslim," he went on to explain, "such an action would constitute the greatest compulsion," a notion which ran contrary to the Revelation which states that "No compulsion is there in religion" (Q.II:256). But unbelievers who consciously took the offensive and encroached upon the *dar al-Islam* would be in an entirely different position.⁶

No longer construed as a just war against the *dar al-harb* on the grounds of disbelief, the duty of the *jihad*, became binding on believers only in the defence of Islam, to be revived by the *Caliph* whenever he believed Islam was in danger. When the Ottoman Empire was established and its Sultans assumed the title of *Caliph*, the *jihad* was often invoked whenever they were involved in a war with the unbelievers. Elated by their victories against the unbelievers in Europe, they turned to eastern Islamic lands and brought them under their

---

5. Sarakhsi, *Kitab al-Mabsut* (Cairo, 1906), Vol. X, pp. 2-3.
6. Ibn Taymiya, "*Qa'ida fi Qital al-Kuffar*", in *Majmu'at Rasa'il*, ed. Marçais (Paris, 1936), p. 15.

control, save Persia which had passed under Shi'i control in the sixteenth century. The Ottoman *Sultan-Caliph* provided leadership to Islamic lands under his control until the fall of the Ottoman Empire following World War I when the *Caliphate* was abolished in 1924.

In theory only the *Caliph*, enthroned to exercise God's sovereignty on Earth, has the power to invoke the *jihad* and call believers to fulfill the duty. Unless the *Caliph* delegates his power to a subordinate governor, nobody has the right to exercise it without prior authorization from him. Were the *jihad* to be proclaimed by any governor without authorization of the *Caliph*, it would be a "secular war" and not a valid or just war. If a dissident leader, whether belonging to an orthodox or heterodox group, claimed the right to declare a *jihad*, his action would be considered disobedience to the *Caliph* and a rebellion against the legitimate authority (Q.XLIX:9).[7] Neither the leader nor the persons who take part in such a *jihad* would be rewarded with Paradise, which is granted only to those who participate in a *jihad* declared by the *Caliph*, the Head of State.

In the dispersed authority of the *Caliphate* throughout Islamic lands first following the fall of the Abbasid dynasty in Baghdad and later after the abolition of the Ottoman *Caliphate*, secular rulers began to exercise civil authority and enforce duties under the law in consultation with the *'ulama'* (religious scholars), but no head of state or political leader could without a religious sanction, claim that he has the power to invoke a just *jihad*. If he were ever involved in fighting, it would be a secular war, but not a *jihad*.

---

7. Shaybani, *The Islamic Law of Nations*, tr. M. Khadduri (Baltimore, 1966), Chap. 8.

Appendix

Constitution of
The Shaybani Society of International Law

Article 1. Name

This Society shall be known as the Shaybani Society of International Law.

Article 2. Objects

The objects of the Society are as follows: (a) to promote the study of Islamic law especially the law relating to the international field; (b) to study Shaybani's works on international law and to encourage their publication; (c) to foster the study of international law relating to the Islamic world; (d) to publish an annual comprising legal studies on the Islamic field.

Article 3. Membership

Membership shall be open to all men and women having interest in the field of legal studies relating to the Islamic world. Membership shall be open to corporations and organizations in a corporate capacity. Dues of membership shall be determined by the Executive Committee.

Article 4

The officers of the Society shall consist of an Honorary President, a President, a Vice President, a Secretary, a Treasurer, and an Executive Committee composed of these officers and members whose number shall be determined from time to time by the President in consultation with the Vice President, Secretary and the Treasurer. All of these officers shall be elected by the members of the Society for a term of four years. The officers shall be elected by a majority vote of the members present and shall serve until their successors are chosen. The functions of the officers shall be to achieve the purposes of the Society by holding periodic meetings as well as by the publication of an annual and other studies. Special committees, whose number and functions are determined by the Executive Committee, shall be organized to achieve in cooperation with the Executive Committee the purposes of the Society.

Article 5. Meetings

At least an annual meeting of the Society shall be held at a time and place to be determined by the Executive Committee. The purposes of the meetings are the presentation of papers, discussion of subjects relating to the purposes of the Society, and to conduct the business of the Society. Special meetings may be held on the call of the Executive Committee.

Article 6. Amendments

This constitution may be amended at any annual meeting of the Society by a two-thirds vote of the members present and voting. Amendments may be proposed either by the Executive Committee or by a written request signed by at least ten members of the Society and submitted through the Secretary so as to be considered by the Executive Committee before the annual meeting.